THE DESIGNER'S
WEB HANDBOOK

what you need to know to create for the web

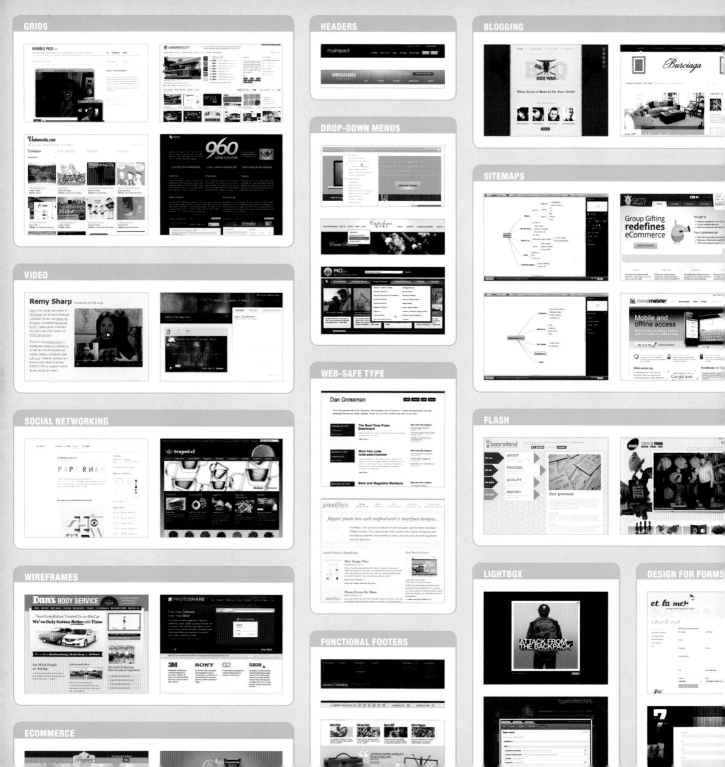

THE DESIGNER'S
WEB HANDBOOK

what you need to know to create for the web

PATRICK McNEIL, bestselling author of *The Web Designer's Idea Book* series

HOW
BOOKS
Cincinnati, Ohio
www.howdesign.com

For more excellent books and resources for designers, visit www.howdesign.com.

16 15 14 13 12   5 4 3 2 1

ISBN-13: 978-1-4403-1441-4

Distributed in Canada by Fraser Direct
100 Armstrong Avenue
Georgetown, Ontario, Canada L7G 5S4
Tel: (905) 877-4411

Distributed in the U.K. and Europe by F&W Media International, LTD
Brunel House, Forde Close, Newton Abbot, TQ12 4PU, UK
Tel: (+44) 1626 323200, Fax: (+44) 1626 323319
Email: enquiries@fwmedia.com

Distributed in Australia by Capricorn Link
P.O. Box 704, Windsor, NSW 2756 Australia
Tel: (02) 4577-3555

Original text for the WordPress appendix courtesy of Jesse Friedman © 2011
Original text for the DPI appendix courtesy of Ben Gremillion © 2011

Edited by Amy Owen
Designed by Grace Ring
Production coordinated by Greg Nock

DEDICATION

For Angela, a relentless supporter

ABOUT THE AUTHOR

Patrick McNeil is a writer, programmer and design lover. His passion for functional, beautiful and engaging design, combined with a lifelong passion for technology, makes the web his favorite playground. While Patrick loves coding and building sites, he equally loves analyzing and working with design. In his ideal world, beautiful design inspires elegant technical solutions; ultimately the combination of these two trades makes for the world's best websites. Driven by an obsession with beautiful design, Patrick works tirelessly to provide designers with the inspiration, challenging ideas and insights to engage the web in meaningful and useful ways.

ACKNOWLEDGMENTS

A book like this is not created in a bubble and is really a byproduct of the influence of my peers, coworkers and the incredible designers that inspire me every day. I sincerely appreciate the countless designers who create the most inspiring and beautiful websites we use each day. I also want to thank the team at F+W, especially Grace and Amy. They not only put a beautiful skin on my books but also transform them into more than I could ever hope them to be. Many thanks to the contributors, especially Jesse for always being willing to jump in and help out. Finally, where would I be without my family? My wife, in particular, has been a relentless supporter, and were it not for her, this book would never have seen the light of day.

THE CONTRIBUTORS

Many thanks to my guest contributors, Jesse Friedman and Ben Gremillion. Each of them provided an appendix for the back of this book. I think you will find the insights they provide to be truly valuable, especially in the context of this book. I want to thank these two for being a part of this project!

Table of Contents

Introduction

Before we dive into this book, I would first like to set in place some fundamental expectations and boundaries for what this book endeavors to accomplish. The intention of this book is to help designers gain an understanding of how the web works and how their designs are ultimately implemented. Through this, designers will be able to predict and appreciate the impact their design has on the full life cycle of a website. By doing so, designers will be able to escape the creative bubble in which they often exist and begin to design sites with a more holistic view.

I like to compare this to oil painting, a topic many creatives can more easily identify with. A budding painter simply attempts to control the paint on a paintbrush. Eventually the artist matures and can control things well enough that he starts asking questions: How does the type of canvas I use impact the painting? What impact does the primer have on the life of a canvas? What impact does it have on how the painting will look? What are the various solutions I can use to impact the consistency of my paint and how it looks on the canvas?

These, and countless other questions, essentially dive into the technical details of oil painting. These technical issues are the limitations the artist works with, regardless of how aware of them he is. These limitations will often frustrate the new painter until he begins to understand them and thereby make sense of the limitations he has been working with. In the end, it is up to the creativity of the artist to work the medium in unique and beautiful ways. But the fundamental limitations of the medium cannot be escaped.

This parallels very well the intentions of this book and how web design works. I seek to educate creatives on what might be considered a digital medium. By fully understanding all the limitations, strengths and weaknesses of the web, one can begin to work *with* it and not *against* it. This is not about holding creatives back, but rather allowing them to unleash their full potential. I am a believer in the cliché, "Knowledge is power." In this case, knowledge of the medium empowers the creative to make informed decisions and ultimately provide more value to their employers and clients.

I also want to be sure to mention what this book is not. This book will not teach you how to code. There are more than enough books on such topics. I will, however, point you in the right direction whenever possible. Also, this book will not teach you how to actually design anything. I will not be spelling out for you what makes a design beautiful.

It should also be said that in many cases this book will serve as a launching point for topics outside the scope of our exploration. As much as possible I will point you to additional resources to implement certain topics or learn about them in greater detail. With a holistic view in mind, it is impossible to dig into every topic in depth. This is also where the online extension of this book plays a huge role. Be sure to register for access to additional and up-to-date resources related to the various topics presented here.

A WORD FROM THE AUTHOR

This book is the culmination of countless conversations, many presentations and an ongoing effort to guide designers into web design. For years I have worked to help designers understand how the web works, how to design for it effectively and how to plan and build websites. I believe that the better you know the medium, the more effective you can be as a designer. And frankly speaking, the more effective you are, the more valuable you are.

You will find that many of the sections in this book will require further reading, and this is by design. With many of the topics presented here, I am only able to scratch the surface, and as such, further reading may be necessary. However, the information given here should help you place the topic in the overall context of designing and building websites. I highly encourage you to explore the topics that impact you most by reading beyond this book.

More than anything, I sincerely hope this book helps you to understand the web. I hope that it helps you to work with the developers you might feel come from a different planet and who certainly speak a different language. And finally, I hope that you will find the web to be an engaging and fulfilling medium, capable of first-class design.

The web is one of the most incredible media ever created, and the more designers understand it, the more exciting I believe they will find it to be. Though, to fully understand the web may seem impossible; I for one have spent a decade trying to do so. In the end, I realize I will never learn all there is to know. This is part of the charm of the web, though. If you thrive on learning, trying new things, experimenting and working in a community, then you will find the web a wonderful place to work. Incidentally, I believe those are many of the traits that creatives hold near to their hearts.

NOTE: Be sure to register at TheDesignersWebHandbook.com for free and exclusive access to even more great tools and resources to help you make the most of the web. If you would like to submit your designs for use in my next book, please visit TheDesignersWebHandbook.com to sign up for my mailing list. You will be informed of book releases, calls for entries and other information directly related to the books. Submitting your sites is free, easy to do and open to everyone. And if you think you are too small of a shop to submit your work, I encourage you to do so anyway. Take pride in showcasing what is happening on the web. In many ways, it is the small shops like yours that come to shape the web.

CHAPTER 1

Usability

THE FORCE THAT BINDS

Usability is the single most defining aspect of the web.

This is a really bold statement, so I want to explain it clearly. The web is a medium that is intended to be interacted with, and every aspect of the web relates back to how it will be used. Therefore, how can we design effective websites if we are not carefully considering usability at every step of the process?

While this book is by no means focused on usability, it is a topic that serves as a great introduction to learning how to design for and work with the web. This is a critical point to consider, as it is a driving force behind almost every topic in this book. If it's not practical and usable, our design has no hope of succeeding and the website ends up as nothing more than a pretty picture (at best).

WHAT IS USABILITY?

So what exactly is usability? Usability is the practice of ensuring that a website is able to accomplish its intended purpose. Even more so, usability implies a pursuit for design that not only accomplishes its goals but also does so in the easiest, clearest way possible. After all, even a horribly architected site can accomplish its goals. Essentially, usability is taking into consideration how the end product will actually be used. Many people like to draw parallels between the web and print and then also draw the contrasts there, but I think a far better comparison is to industrial design.

Consider automotive design. Every aspect of a vehicle is designed from the points of view of both aesthetics and usability (not to mention the technical implications, but more on that later). What if an automotive designer decided the door handles looked far cooler at the bottom of the door? Not so cool when your hands are full of groceries.

Good usability can be the difference between a huge success and a complete failure. Imagine the possibilities if you combine beautiful design *and* usability principles!

MORE THAN GOOD LOOKS

The real irony is that a design can be beautiful and yet a horrible failure in terms of usability. I have seen countless comps that look fantastic hanging on the wall as a printout during a group critique. But in the end they simply don't function; they fall short once built because they lack an attention to usability. If you are to succeed as a web designer, your first consideration should be usability.

We have to let go of the thought that our creativity is of primary importance. We are not here to create works of art but rather to solve client problems through functional solutions that meet real business needs.

This doesn't mean you have to put aside all that creative energy you have. If anything, it means the total opposite. All I am suggesting is that there are some practical guidelines to operate within. Just like with any skill, once you master the rules you can break them in so many ways.

SAVE MONEY AND BUILD VALUE

Usability is about more than just defining rules for the designer; it actually saves time and builds value for your clients. When we consider usability as a core factor in all that we do, we help ensure that what we deliver to our clients will function well and reach their audience. Please don't confuse reaching an audience with using appropriate images, language and styles. This is about reaching them in the sense that the site successfully engages them—and ideally results in a planned response.

Considering usability can easily save money by ensuring we get the website design right the first time, so it doesn't need to be rebuilt or redesigned. But even more so, good usability can increase the revenue produced by a site. On an e-commerce site, this is a direct correlation, so in such cases usability is always a central topic when designers and clients sit down to discuss project goals. But consider a standard brochure site; good usability in terms of finding a "request a quote" form and then good usability on the actual form can maximize the amount of people that take that step to contact the company. This would mean more sales leads, and most likely more sales.

When you consider all of your clients' problems with a focus on usability, you are really helping them to better meet their customers' needs, and in the end they will love you for it. This doesn't mean that all along the way you have not been able to produce fresh creative work; it just means you have a greater purpose. And that purpose will make your clients happy—and happy clients are typically repeat customers and great referrers of more business.

IT'S ALL ABOUT USABILITY

To be realistic, I haven't said anything about usability in terms of how to actually practice it. And this is essentially what the rest of the book is for. Though I might not directly connect topics back to usability, they almost all relate back to it in some way, and it is a common theme in almost everything web designers and developers touch.

Constantly ask yourself, "How will this be used?"

USABILITY RESOURCES

If you would like to dig into the topic of usability in depth, here are some helpful resources to get you started.

http://52weeksofux.com
This usability resource covers a new topic each week. The site is incredibly rich with insights that will totally transform the way you design. Stick with it and read this site over the course of a year to get the most out of it.

www.useit.com
Jakob Nielsen is perhaps the king of usability. His research and resulting articles contain information that would be very expensive and time consuming to

acquire on our own. Don't be misled by the simplicity (and perhaps ugliness) of his site; the content contained in it is priceless. Fortunately, some of it is free.

www.usability.gov

If you would like to see what the U.S. government has to say about usability, this is the easiest way to get to the source of things. You might be surprised to find that there are laws that govern the usability of certain types of sites. If you find yourself on a publicly funded project, you should get familiar with this resource.

CHAPTER 2

Starting a New Project

So, let's start from the beginning and work our way through the various stages of a project. The first stage is the acceptance of a new project. This starts in the sales process and continues into the start of the actual project.

LISTEN AND CONSIDER BUSINESS LOGIC

Before we do anything, we absolutely have to listen to the client. It can be so easy to make assumptions or to come to our own conclusions about what a client needs. And at times we are right and it is the wise thing to speak up. But before that, just be quiet and listen to the client. Quite often I find that you can figure out in the very first conversations what will make the client extremely happy. More often than not, the problems that plague a customer are basic and present targets that can easily be addressed. If we pay attention, we will discover the nuggets that they are looking for.

I encourage you to dig deep with your clients and ask as many questions as you can. The more you understand the problems they are facing, the better equipped you will be to help them succeed. One thing that will inevitably come up very early on is the type of project they are in need of.

DETERMINE YOUR SITE TYPE

Once you discover the type of project you are working with, you can start to ask some good questions that will provide you valuable insights into the project. Let's look at some key considerations regarding planning a project, depending on the type of project, with the goal being to get you thinking about the impact the type of site has on the project. This is by no means an all-inclusive listing of the possibilities, but it should get you thinking about the range of things to consider.

BROCHURE SITES

The standard brochure site is perhaps the simplest of sites. (See page 013 for samples.) Anyone who's conducted any kind of business on the Internet can likely guess some of the basic content that will show up (about us, contact form, products and services, etc.). On a site like this, one of the biggest considerations is simply how much content or how many pages there are. More pages mean more money.

Ask the client if they have a sitemap prepared, as this will help you understand the scope of the project. It is very unlikely they will have one, and a client that does have one is a good client. A sitemap sketches out what you will build so the client knows exactly what they are buying. This also helps you later on when they ask about something that wasn't in the plan, making it much easier to charge appropriately for the additional work. (See the section called "Make a Sitemap" on page 036 in this chapter.)

Another common concern for customers is updating the site. In this case, clients need to understand that a content management system (CMS) is required (more on these in the CMS section in chapter four on page 097). CMSes are great in that they make it easy for a client to update a site without having to call you for support (with additional billable hours). On the other hand, it will cost them more up front to build the site. All the same, clients typically want to be able to update their site and save some money in the long run.

E-COMMERCE SITES

Everyone seems to want to sell something online; the problem is that one of the most complex types of sites to work on are e-commerce ones. (See page 014 for samples.) There are just so many moving parts, including credit-card processing, email sub systems and product photography, to name a few.

The biggest hurdle for most e-commerce projects is that content management is far more time consuming than building the site. It takes a remarkable amount of time to populate a system with even a small number of products. And generating or acquiring quality photography is exceedingly involved and very expensive.

On an e-commerce project you will really benefit from a close relationship with a developer who can handle a lot of the heavy technical

BROCHURE SITES

www.doublediamondmoving.com

1 This standard brochure site primarily consists of static content geared at selling their services, much like a physical brochure might do.

2 While it looks nothing like a brochure, the static nature of this restaurant site is to provide users with the basic information they need.

3 The brochure-type approach of this site is easy to maintain and has a long potential life, ensuring it is not expensive to maintain and update.

www.fullmoonbbq.com

http://alexanderhomesteadweddings.com

E-COMMERCE SITES

1 This e-commerce site doesn't fit the traditional mold and demonstrates that there is still plenty of room for creativity within the bounds of an e-commerce system.

2 The sales process on this e-commerce site doesn't fit the norms, but it sells the product extremely well. Keep in mind that sites such as this are extremely customized and are far from inexpensive.

3 This simple one-page e-commerce site serves up a single product. Keeping the exact needs of a site in mind can often result in unexpected results such as this.

www.doopsuikerpoppies.be

http://www.moo.com

http://getconcentrating.com

work. Even if you use a hosted platform that doesn't require you to install it, typically there are still a lot of technical gotchas to deal with.

There is almost no way in the world you will be involved in building a ground-up e-commerce solution, given the range of quality off-the-shelf systems available. As such, the E-Commerce section regarding CMS selection in chapter four on page 103 will really help you understand what you're in for.

Finally, as the designer, you need to know that e-commerce projects often require ongoing involvement. In addition, it is very seldom that a creative can accommodate *all* the elements that are needed when it comes to e-commerce. For some clues as to all of the elements you will need, look in the E-Commerce section in chapter five on page 162.

ENTERTAINMENT SITES

If you find yourself looking down the barrel of an entertainment-related site, you're most likely facing a promotion, an online game, a site to represent a game, a movie site or a site for a band. (See page 017 for samples.) As a creative you are in luck; these are some of the types of sites that are more tolerant of pushing the envelope. In such cases there is a focus on the experience and at times it seems that usability and all sense of practicality can be pushed out the window.

It is in these situations that understanding what works well in terms of usability is powerful because you can stick close to practical principles, while introducing some creative approaches. The best sites of this type retain a sense of usability, while still creating a really unique experience.

This type of site is also one of the most common places to find an all-Flash solution. While Flash might not be as popular as it once was, it is still incredibly powerful, and entertainment-related sites are one place it excels. Keep in mind that these sorts of sites can be pricey and very time consuming to build.

Another common element with entertainment sites is the "throw away" factor. Quite often sites such as these are considered a one-off project that will require only light updates, if any. Sites like these either disappear after a few years (or less), or are simply replaced to be in line with current trends.

NEWS SITES

Most news sites are handled by internal teams, but if you find that you're talking with a client about what you would consider a news site (perhaps for a TV news show or something along those lines) there are probably going to be two key things to consider. (See page 018 for samples.)

The first is advertising. News sites of all shapes and sizes are almost always jam-packed with advertising. In such cases, a third-party component or software will be priceless in helping your client manage the flow of ads. Address this issue and you will likely find that your client loves you.

Second, news sites must be updated very frequently. As such, a strong CMS will need to be in place to handle the flow of content. Be sure to check the CMS section in chapter four on page 097 for some potential solutions.

http://holyrollersfilm.com

1 Notice that while this site has a creative layer to it, the fundamental goal is to communicate all of the critical information: title, trailers, cast, news and social media, for example.

2 Band sites are the modern equivalent of the album cover and typically communicate a band's style and hopefully resonate well with the artist's music.

3 Short-lived websites such as this often leave lots of room for creativity since the goal is to hook users and not to build a long-living website.

www.ryanedgarmusic.com

www.bloedoranjegallery.com

NEWS SITES

1 This news-type site demonstrates that news comes in many forms, from TV to blogs. The basic needs are very much the same, though, and are typically driven by ad sales, which in this case are very tastefully done.

www.bloggercore.com

BLOGS

Given the immense popularity of blogs, it won't take long for you to run into a project where you need to skin a blog. (See page 020 for samples.) As with many of the other topics here, the CMS section will be of great help; look to page 100 in chapter four for more info regarding the topic.

During the sales process, though, there are a few things to be aware of that are specific to blog projects.

First, if you're building a blog, you will be using a piece of software like WordPress or Posterous to do so. This means you will either need to be familiar with such software or have a developer working on the project who is. This is very important because a site can be integrated on a platform to varying degrees of effectiveness. You will want your client to be able to easily manage the site once it's up and running, so hiring a developer who can effectively skin the application is invaluable.

The second consideration is that your client needs to be aware that maintenance of a blog is far greater of a concern then designing and building one. Blogs require constant attention. The blog's administrator must research new content, write articles, interact with the audience and promote the blog. It turns into a lot of work very quickly. It is wise to make sure your client is up for this. Again, expressing your concern for their long-term cost of ownership typically resonates very well with clients.

BLOGS

1 While this blog follows the standard physical layout, it has a beautiful and custom style that sets it apart. The balance between beauty, functionality and practicality is perfect here.

2 This popular web design blog focuses on the flow of new content, the lifeblood of a blog.

3 This niche-focused blog follows the norms while relying on a distinct and memorable style.

www.inspiredology.com

www.webdesignerdepot.com

http://freelanceswitch.com

COMMUNITY SITES

If I scared you a little with my comments regarding the maintenance of a blog (and I hope I did at least a little bit), then I really want to scare some sense into you about the work a community site requires.

The owners of a community site are in store for a rude awakening if they think they can casually launch a community site and it will just take off and run itself. Such sites require constant babysitting. The startup is also the most painful time. Your client will need to pour time and energy into getting it rolling with what will often feel like a very small return. It just takes time to really get community sites ramped up and going. Prepare them for the workload, help them plan content and make sure they are prepared to hurry up and wait.

Another huge consideration is that a community site is going to include tons of dynamic content and will border on being nothing more than a specific type of application (see the section on applications on page 023). With that in mind, carefully consider the usability of your design and its flexibility for ever-changing content.

EDUCATIONAL SITES

Education sites (and higher education sites, specifically) almost always share one fundamental problem: design by committee. (See page 022 for samples.) There are exceptions to this, so I don't want to overgeneralize, but chances are you won't be so lucky. It is almost inevitable that a group of people with disparate agendas will be providing insight into the design needs of the project at hand. As a designer, you likely don't need me to explain to you why this is a horrible scenario. All the

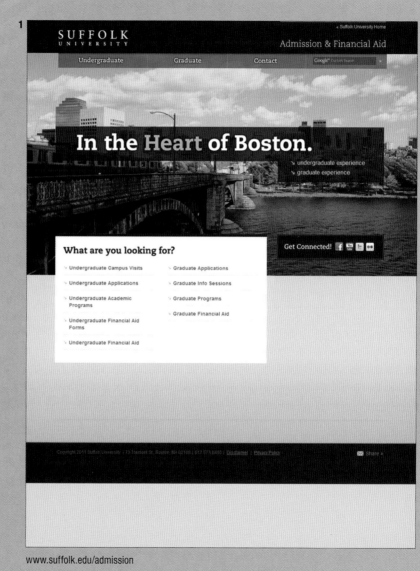

1 Educational sites can be a tremendous challenge, and this makes successful sites such as this one all the more impressive.

www.suffolk.edu/admission

same, if you expect to report to a committee instead of an individual, it will help you plan your expectations for the project.

Another very common thing with this particular niche is that the types of solutions educational institutions often need are more along the lines of an application. What might appear to be a simple informational site can quickly turn into a full-blown application with all sorts of complex needs directly related to the way the business runs. Check out the applications section below for considerations if this happens.

APPLICATIONS

Web applications are turning into a huge industry. (See page 025 for samples.) Many web applications are starting to displace desktop software. This marks an exciting time on the web as these applications change the ways businesses work. Frankly speaking, though, as a designer, running into a potential application design project should bring up some very real red flags. Here are the top three things you should keep in mind.

Above all else, designing applications is vastly different from designing your run-of-the-mill promotional site. Applications are far less about the clever styles you can apply and almost entirely about usability. Sure, they have to look nice. But in the end if you don't carefully think through the design and how it will actually function, you are going to have a very unhappy client on your hands. Approach this type of project with caution, as there are designers who dedicate their entire careers to mastering the design of applications.

Next, you should pay careful attention to how organized and prepared your client is. If the application is still a vague idea and they don't have concrete plans in place, it is going to be very difficult to pin down a price point. If your client is trying to contract out design work related to such a project, they should at least have sitemaps and flowcharts for how the application will function and what it will do. Without these you have no idea what you're designing.

Finally, don't expect to deliver your assets and walk away from a project like this. There is almost no way in the world you can account for everything that will be needed. As such, try to get your client to budget for a bit of follow-up work so you can help them polish the project with assets that were not planned for.

MOBILE DEVICES

If one thing has become abundantly clear, it's that we can no longer ignore the mobile web. This includes tablets as well as smart phones. If you find yourself on a project targeted at mobile devices, you should know that sites for mobile devices (not apps) can be built using standard CSS and HTML technologies. These core technologies are the basic building blocks of the web and the lifeblood of web designers and front-end developers. The one gotcha is that mobile-targeted development comes with it all sorts of nuances that are not universally known.

So, if you want to make the most of an opportunity such as this, you will really want to make sure you have a development team up to the task. And on the design side, you will really have to be aware of the constraints, norms and usability concerns of mobile design.

From a pricing standpoint, such projects can range as widely as any other website. Perhaps the biggest gotcha is if a client wants a

WEB APPLICATIONS

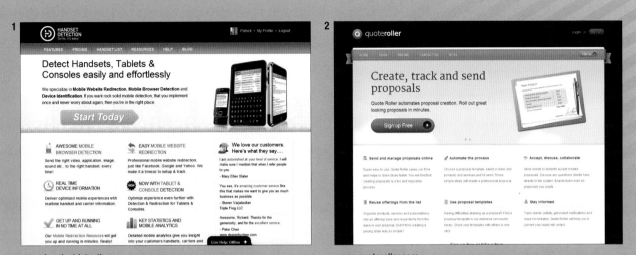

www.handsetdetection.com

www.quoteroller.com

http://network.operationshower.org

1 Sites that promote an application are just as important as the actual app. This site clearly communicates the function of the service and entices you to take a test drive.

2 This is another gorgeous app site that clearly communicates and sells the product effectively. I particularly like how the style of the site resonates with the design quality of the digital proposals.

3 This application interface is very modular—a common approach to building web apps, as it allows for lots of flexibility and change over time.

HYBRID SITES

1 Many websites blend the various approaches together and result in a wide variety of creations. This sample provides a portal to the different components and is easily updated. It's a fantastic solution for a dynamic site that has to change constantly.

2 This site combines many types of sites into a single entity. This is really hard to pull off, as it typically means combining several systems. This gorgeous site makes it look easy.

3 This standard-looking site combines static content, e-commerce and blogging. Merging these elements is critical to a smooth client interaction.

www.cheshirescouts.org.uk

http://drleaf.com

http://themes.bavotasan.com

website that is also appropriate for the mobile web. Keep in mind that this is more like building two websites. As such, the price should reflect this.

HYBRID SITES

In reality, almost every project will be a hybrid of the types of sites previously mentioned (and many other types I don't have room to include). (See page 026 for samples.) This is normal and a benefit of the way the web fundamentally works. In so many ways, web development is more about trying all sorts of stuff until it works than anyone ever really admits. So mixing styles of sites is to be expected. It's actually half the fun of working with the web.

CONCLUSION

I know this is a lot of information regarding the various types of sites—especially since we are still in the project-planning phase. But I think you will find that your projects will go far better if you begin each new site by carefully considering its purpose and the type of content it will host. Hopefully these pointers will help you understand what you are in for on a project and help you intelligently guide your clients to the best possible solutions.

CONDUCT A DESIGN SURVEY

An invaluable part of the planning phase for any project will be a general design survey. At this point, you should do everything you can to be a master of a few key things.

First, consider the client's tastes. A natural part of the planning phase will be discussing your client's particular tastes in web design. Get samples from them of sites they love and hate, and from there, branch out to find as many more sites as you can that fit those styles. The more you see what others are doing in those particular styles the better.

You should also shop the competition. I suppose it goes without saying, but you simply have to look at what your client's competitors are up to and how their sites look. This will not only provide you with insight into what customers in the niche might expect, but it will hopefully highlight some weaknesses and holes that you can help your client fill.

And of course, your design exposure should not be limited to this part of the process. I highly encourage you to build a pattern of cataloguing design elements you love or find useful. I also encourage you to consume as much quality web design content as you can. There are literally hundreds of web design showcases with an equally wide range of focuses. Below I will highlight some of the most powerful tools in my arsenal for staying current on design trends.

RESOURCES

Evernote
www.evernote.com
This handy tool is the modern equivalent of filling shoeboxes with cool stuff that inspires you. You can capture text, images and audio clips. Each snippet gets a tag and a primary category. Over time, you can amass a library of inspiring snippets. This tool is exceptionally handy in that you can use it on a computer or mobile device.

The CSS Awards

www.awwwards.com

This web design showcase is notable for its high-quality content, due in no small part to its thorough jury process. You can be certain that any site found here represents the current styles in web design and is top notch.

CSS Remix

http://cssremix.com

This gallery is another all-around showcase that features a flow of fantastic sites. And as the name not so subtly suggests, it features sites built primarily using CSS. As such, it is a great way to get a constant stream of sites using modern HTML/CSS techniques.

Favorite Website Awards

www.thefwa.com

This site has been around for a really long time and contains what is more than likely the largest and highest quality repository of Flash-based sites. If you are even remotely interested in seeing what can be done with Flash, this is the first place to stop. This site makes it easy to love Flash, as there is absolutely amazing work being done with it.

Pattern Tap

http://patterntap.com

Instead of showing a general flow of cool sites, Pattern Tap collects snippets of sites based on functionality. This resource is priceless when it comes to researching various ways to design the building blocks of a page.

INSPIRATION RESOURCES

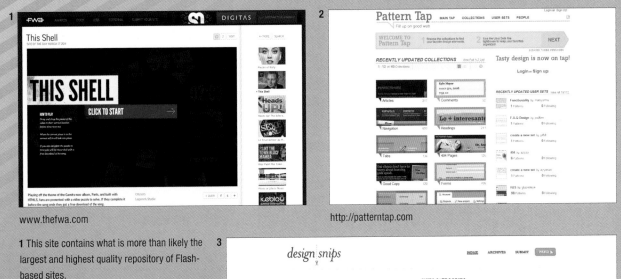

1 www.thefwa.com

2 http://patterntap.com

1 This site contains what is more than likely the largest and highest quality repository of Flash-based sites.

2 This resource is priceless when it comes to researching various ways to design the building blocks of a page.

3 This site focuses on collecting sites and elements that match various design styles.

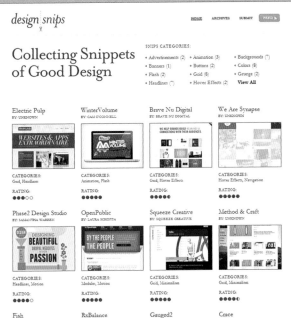

3 www.designsnips.com

Design Snips
http://designsnips.com

This site takes a similar approach to Pattern Tap except that it focuses on collecting sites and elements that match various design styles. Again, this can be incredibly helpful when you are looking for creative ways to handle a particular element of a page.

Mobile Awesomeness
www.mobileawesomeness.com

As mobile development becomes more and more commonplace, design showcases like this one that feature mobile sites and applications are helpful for staying current. Mobile design is constantly evolving, and using sites like this one to eliminate the need to browse a lot on your mobile device is a real time saver.

iOSpirations
www.iospirations.com

In this mobile showcase, you will find a nice mix of iPhone- and iPad-style sites and apps. Resources like this let you begin to get acclimated to these ever-evolving media, without the need to purchase the devices. Start your research now, because mobile design projects are only getting more common.

BEN: Beautiful Email Newsletters
www.beautiful-email-newsletters.com

HTML emails play a huge role in the web industry. This great site showcases lots of beautiful emails. I can't even begin to express how tremendously helpful it is to have a collection like this out there.

Without it, it would be nearly impossible to see a good range of email designs without putting in a ton of research work.

Motionspire
http://motionspire.com

For a bit of inspiration a step outside of the web, take a look at Motionspire. This site showcases a fantastic flow of motion graphics. Never underestimate the power of looking at industries outside the web for a bit of fresh inspiration. This site will make you want to change careers.

CartFrenzy
http://cartfrenzy.com

There is a gallery for almost every niche, but e-commerce is one that really needs it. E-commerce design is some of the most complex web work a designer can get involved in, so resources like CartFrenzy can really help us see creative things others are doing with sites like this.

Grid-Based Designs
www.grid-based.com

Grid-based design is such a common concept in print, yet many designers making the move to the web leave it behind. Dig into this site and you will quickly find that grid-based design is a powerful tool in the designer's arsenal.

ESTABLISH BENCHMARKS

Planning a web project will involve some basic benchmarking. This is the sort of thing that often happens on a natural level and no one

MORE INSPIRATION RESOURCES

www.beautiful-email-newsletters.com

1 Without this site, it would be nearly impossible to see a good range of email designs without putting in a ton of research work.

2 This site showcases a fantastic flow of motion graphics.

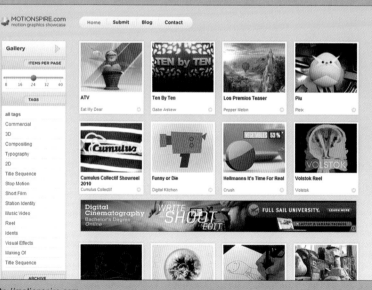

http://motionspire.com

really calls it out for what it is. But let's not take anything for granted. Benchmarking is simply the process of researching the competition, the industry in general and the specific goals of the client we are working with. Let's dig into each of these topics individually.

RESEARCHING THE COMPETITION

How can we build a site for a new client without putting in some effort to assess what the competition is up to? Surprisingly, this step is often missed. The best way to address the issue is to ask the client directly who their competition is. I have had many situations where the client's whole goal was to squash their rather clear competitors.

The next part of this is researching the competition online. Oftentimes, clients will have competition they don't even know about. Perhaps some other shop has figured out how to leverage the web and has jumped ahead of them. Regardless, you need to know where the client stands in contrast to their competition.

This helps immerse you in the client's industry. You will really start to understand what they do or sell, and working with them will only get more comfortable as you understand how the industry they are in works. Even better, you can start to spot opportunities and weaknesses that the competition has yet to address. This is yet another great way to bring real value to your customers.

TECHNOLOGY STANDARDS

During the process of investigating the competition, pay careful attention to the technologies they use. This will begin to demonstrate to you what their customers have come to expect. Is video a common factor? Perhaps social networking is more important than expected in the niche. Or maybe the technology is archaic and borderline painful to use.

The best place to start is by reviewing any web analytics the client might already have (based on current site traffic). If this is an option, be sure to get access. Analytics can tell you all sorts of things: Where does the majority of traffic come from (geographically speaking)? What web browsers are predominately used? Are mobile devices hitting the client's site? All of these things help you form a general idea of the target audience.

Put this data together and you have a formula for assessing the norms and expectations in the industry, as well as a clear view of the technological capabilities within the client's current audience. From there, you can make very strategic decisions in terms of your suggestions for the project. I can't lay out a plan for you in this area, though; it is so different in every case. But I find that by doing the two things listed here, obvious opportunities will present themselves.

GOALS AND OBJECTIVES

How can we pretend to understand a client's needs without setting some goals and objectives? Again, this borders on stating the obvious, but as you consider it more carefully, it's another planning element that is ignored more often than not.

By understanding the goals a client has, we simply have a better chance at succeeding. Just ask the client, "What do you want to accomplish with this new site?" You might get something as generic as "we want to attract more customers," but push for something deeper than that. *How* do they want to grow their business (because that is pretty much what everyone wants and what everyone says at first)? Do they want to grow their email marketing list? Do they want to start an email marketing list? Do they want to increase their sales leads to increase revenue? Do they need to better handle customer service issues so as to save on overhead costs? A fabulous question for you to ask your client at this point is, "What would make this project a success to you?" It is such digging that will give you a far better understanding of how to approach the project. Frankly, if you don't ask questions like this, you're just taking stabs in the dark—with your client footing the bill.

MAKE A SITEMAP

A crucial part of the planning process is the sitemap. A sitemap is nothing more than a plan for how all of the various pages of a site will be organized. This does not account for all the cross linking that might happen, but rather it focuses on the fundamental organizational structure of the site. Sitemaps can be a tremendous aid to everyone involved in a web project, yet they are all too often left out. Let's look at some of the benefits that come with them.

The benefits of creating a sitemap begin in the bidding process of a website. By taking the time to nail down all of the content that will be included in the site, as well as the critical elements of the site, you will find that everyone has a much clearer picture of the end product. First you will be able to far more accurately bid the work. By simply knowing what the site will contain, you can make a far more informed pricing decision. This leads to another huge upside to using a sitemap: Later on in the project, if the client says something

SAMPLE SITEMAP

1 This sample sitemap demonstrates the contents of a site and provides a clear view of the entire project to minimize confusion.

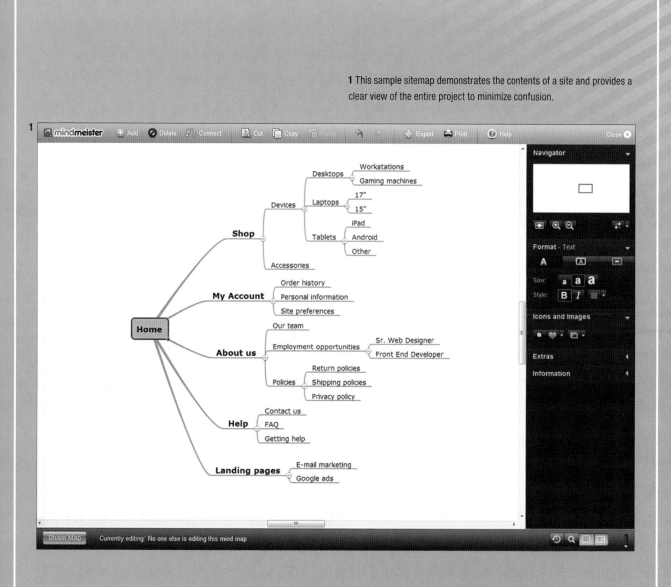

ANOTHER SAMPLE SITEMAP

www.giftsproject.com

1 This is a website I chose to use as a reference point for creating another sample sitemap.

2 This sample sitemap for the website The Gifts Project demonstrates the clarity and usefulness of a sitemap. This is a great way to eliminate confusion with clients over what is to be built.

to the effect of, "So, where is section X?" (with X being a previously unmentioned section of the site that would increase the total project scope by 25 percent), you can easily price out the extra elements and generate a paid work order. If, on the other hand, you simply told the client, "We will build you a $10,000 website," well, you're kind of stuck and are forced to make changes and additions until their hearts are content. Sitemaps will save you time and time again.

In a bit of a more hands-on way, sitemaps help you, the designer, when it comes time to put pixels in place. One of the first questions that will likely come up during the design phase is, "What content goes into the site?" Well, with a sitemap in place it is pretty clear. You know what navigation elements to include. You will find yourself very well informed in regard to what you are designing. The sitemap will save everyone the time of relaying information as the project moves down the pipeline. This benefit goes all the way to the developer at the end of the line building the site. He may have had little to no contact with the client or the project in general. The sitemap helps to quickly and painlessly communicate the plan to him as he builds the site out.

MINDMEISTER

www.mindmeister.com

I have worked with many tools to generate sitemaps, and MindMeister is by far the simplest and fastest tool I have found. You can generate a sitemap in record time (leav-

ing you no excuse not to). Even better, you can come back and edit it just as easily. Don't fuss with Illustrator or Photoshop for sitemaps when a tool like this is available.

MindMeister also offers up versions to run locally on your computer as well as on iPhones and iPads. This makes it really easy to merge this handy tool into your typical workflow.

This tool actually goes beyond sitemaps, once you get hooked on it. It is fantastic for planning anything out. I have planned out dozens of screencasts for tutorials and articles, or just a collection of random business ideas. This book was originally mapped out in MindMeister, in fact.

CREATE A WIREFRAME

We can't possibly mention sitemaps without pulling wireframes into the mix. Wireframes are like blueprints for individual pages of a site. A wireframe will carefully plan out the content and functionality of a page without addressing any real design issues. Typically these are done in black and white and with very generic layout tools. This intentionally keeps the customer from focusing on design issues.

The goal is to wireframe key pages and layouts of a site. By doing so, you can work out with a client a lot of the changes that would typically take place after the client has seen the initial comps. This approach brings us back to the topic of usability. If we take the time to carefully plan out the wireframes for a site, we are forced to consider key client objectives and the overall usability of our layout. And since we're not dealing with a polished design, making changes is not painful or time consuming.

Many people think wireframes are like a rough sketch or general idea that gives the designer some general direction. That's true in the general sense, but I would argue that if you take the time to work with your clients on wireframes, you will find that they become very much like the blueprints for a house. A blueprint for a house might not tell you what color the walls are or what type of counter tops you will have, but they do tell you how the site will function, how it fits together and how the different areas flow together. This is a perfect analogy to planning a website.

WIREFRAMES

ProtoShare
www.protoshare.com
Some interesting new tools have emerged in the wireframe niche. ProtoShare transforms the process of creating wireframes from being simply static images to look at. Instead, this tool lets you build pages in wireframe style that actually func-

tion. It generates the code for you to create live wireframes that users can click through and test drive. Depending on the scale of your project, this can be a fabulous tool.

Adobe Photoshop
www.photoshop.com

In case you were wondering, making wireframes inside Photoshop is not only reasonable, but it can also actually be very beneficial. Imagine that you make your Photoshop-based wireframes at the appropriate size for the web so that they are true to form in terms of scale. This means that once you go to design, you are literally designing over the top of your wireframe that is sized perfectly. By having the wireframe all ready in Photoshop, you can save time and ensure that the result matches the wireframe very accurately.

PRESENT ONE COMP

As I consider and observe the planning process that leads up to a web project, I can't help but ponder the typical practice of presenting the client with three comps to pick from. I have worked in numerous agencies and have experienced a wide range of planning strategies—from none at all to complete plans from start to finish. One common pattern

I have observed is that the more time that is spent in planning the project, the easier it is to generate a comp that matches the needs and tastes of the client on the first try.

I acknowledge that the approach of only generating a single comp will not work for all websites; for example, promotional sites that are extremely conceptually driven are very much about pitching ideas to the client, not so much a specific project. I am not speaking to such situations.

But what if you planned out your project so well that you found you could nail the client's needs in one comp? There are agencies that do this, and they get a few huge perks that give them a competitive advantage. The biggest of these is that they don't get clients trying to Frankenstein together multiple designs. How often have you had a client ask you to take a piece from each comp and merge them together?

The second big upside is that you can sell this as a benefit to your clients; you can charge less (because you're doing a lot less design work). This makes your price more competitive. Regardless of the state of the economy, this is something that resonates with business owners and is another great way to demonstrate a respect for the client's needs, time and money.

Again, this might not work for everyone, but at least take the time to consider it. It is my belief that this approach is more viable and less used than it should be. But don't just take my opinion; here is a YouTube video of Paul Rand preaching the same thing (he only gave ABC one design option): http://bit.ly/mZoote.

CONCLUSION

This brings us to the end of what I consider the planning phase of any project. At this point, no design or development work has taken place (and often we have to be careful not to have done too much). However, this doesn't mean that all of this work happened before signing a contract. For example, wireframing in particular is something that typically happens after a working contract is in place.

I hope you take the planning phase of a website seriously and I hope this section has provided some valuable insights into how to plan a site, as well as why planning is so critical. I have found this part of the process to be tempting to skip (typically due to overly compressed timelines), but if I do, I always regret it.

CHAPTER 3

Components of Web Pages

A critical aspect of the web for designers to learn is that the web is made up of standard components, or building blocks, that can be used to build websites. To illustrate this point, I am going to make an analogy to the field of architecture.

When an architect sets out to design a house, she does so with an array of standard components to work with:

- Room types, like bedrooms, living rooms and kitchens
- Things to connect them, like stairs, doors and hallways
- Various things to put in those rooms, like closets, sinks, lights, windows and appliances

In this way, the architect sets out to design a house by making use of commonly accepted elements. And, of course, this is not a limitation; it is just a matter of fact that these are the building blocks for a house. At times (on high-end projects), the architect gets to explore some more alternative elements—but this will always impact the final price. Architects don't often invent new ways to get from room to room, or even new types of rooms, just because they are feeling creative.

I think this is a great way to look at the building blocks available to us on the web. These components don't limit the creative potential; they are simply the pieces used to create websites. All too often I encounter resistance from designers on this point; they tend to think I am trying to rein them in. In reality, I am simply showing them the tools they have to work with, and much the same as in architecture, the possibilities are still endless.

A major reason to make use of these commonly accepted components is that they carry a great deal of built-in usability with them. Through repetition, end users have been trained to know what to do when they encounter certain components. It would be foolish to cast aside these learned behaviors in the name of creativity.

Another huge reason to embrace this mind-set is cost. If everything you design for the web requires a developer to jump through major technical hurdles to get something working, the cost of the solutions you design will always be high. Perhaps that is okay, depending on your clients. But I believe that if you really understand your options, you can build functional sites that look amazing, potentially cost your clients less and, even better, allow your agency to turn a greater profit.

Let's dig through a number of these components to see what they do and what they might contain, as well as standard approaches to them and, of course, some samples to look at.

HEADERS

The header of a website is the chunk of content that appears at the top of a site. This component is almost universal, but there are situations in which it can be eliminated. For the most part, though, every site will (or should) have one. There are a number of things that we typically find here:

TOP-LINE BRANDING

We typically find the primary branding for a website in this region. This will often include a sub brand or a tag line of some sort. Most often the logo is in the top left corner, but this is not always true, nor is it required; it's just a common pattern people have come to expect.

PRIMARY NAVIGATION

The primary navigation will typically be connected to the header of the site. This navigation allows users to drill down into various regions of the site. In some cases, the overall page count is low enough that the entirety of the navigation can be contained here in a drop-down menu.

SECONDARY NAVIGATION

Oftentimes a site will separate out a secondary navigation containing items that are not as core to the sales process. Things like About Us and Contact Us often fall here.

SEARCH FUNCTIONALITY

Most often we find a search field in the header. This makes good sense, considering the main navigation can be found here.

ACCOUNT INFORMATION

www.myimpact.co.uk

www.ambassadorsforlife.org

1 This sample site header contains almost all of the standard elements: logo, navigation, secondary links and login options. The only thing missing is a search feature.

2 This is another example of a header packed with many of the most common elements. Notice that following the norms doesn't have to be visually boring.

3 In this case, the header is far less busy and, as a result, very easy to use. The simplicity and clarity ensure users can easily dig into the site without any confusion.

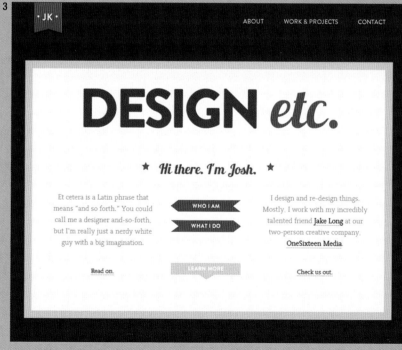

www.joshkennedydesign.com

ACCOUNT INFORMATION

If a site includes a secure section, links to My Account or Log in/Log out options will typically be found here.

There are a lot of elements to think about. And while some sites contain all of these elements, most sites will only require a subset of this list.

NAVIGATION/MENUS

Though I included navigation as an element of the header region, it is really a component all unto its own. There are three primary forms of menu-based navigation. Pretty much everything is a spin-off of these, in one way or another.

TABS

Tabs are typically used as a primary navigation tool to direct people to landing pages for various sections of a site. (See page 050 for samples.) These tabs offer no subnavigation inside of themselves but instead rely on the pages within the tab to handle this.

DROP-DOWN MENUS

Drop-down menus can be horizontal or vertical, though they are most often horizontal. (See page 051 for samples.) These menus typically act in a very predictable way that users understand. Users naturally carry over their experience and understanding of these menus, as they are found in most desktop applications. These menus allow us to quickly drill down to exactly what we are looking for.

TABS

1 Tabbed content such as this allows more content to be contained in a space. Even more so, it allows you to break the content into consumable chunks that help minimize confusion and clutter.

2 Here the tabs help the user visualize the content of the sites in various content sections.

3 Again the tabbed navigation is more to help users understand the site's structure as a sort of folder-based approach.

1

http://openpublicapp.com

2

http://bavotasan.com

3

www.actionforblindpeople.org.uk

DROP-DOWN MENUS

www.webcoursesbangkok.com

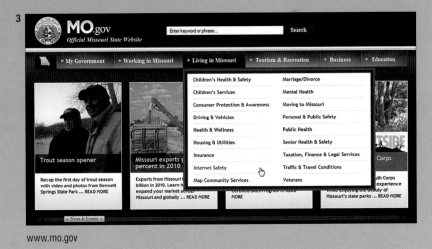

www.carolinagirlevents.com

1 Sometimes keeping it simple is the best approach. This drop-down menu is simple and to the point, though it is carefully crafted to fit the style of the site.

2 Here's another standard implementation of a drop-down menu. Don't lose track of the functional nature of this element. Keeping it clean and easy to use is ideal to ensure users have no problem navigating the site.

3 Many sites will contain so many options that you have to do customized drop-down menus such as this one. A simple two-column approach ensures the list stays on screen.

www.mo.gov

TREES

Tree-based menus are almost always going to be vertical menus, found in one of the sidebars of a layout. I can't say that I have ever seen a horizontal tree menu, so let's assume here that it will be vertical. These tree-type menus can display the full contents of a site or simply a subsection of the current pages. In this way, they can either allow you to drill down or select from a static list of options.

There are many other ways to allow users to browse through content, but I think it is really good to note the most standard ones. I would dare say that 99 percent of sites are built using these. So, if you find yourself using what I would call atypical navigation in all of your comps and getting lukewarm or negative feedback from your client, then you should carefully consider the more commonly accepted means of navigating the web. And, of course, take exception to this feedback if you happen to work in a niche that requires such atypical approaches.

If you're curious how to know if you're using atypical navigation, consider this: If every navigation system you design requires some sort of explanation to the developer as to how it works, then you're probably doing something unusual. The three previously mentioned approaches are commonly accepted and simply don't require explanation.

FOOTERS

Footers tend to fall into one of two categories: functional navigational tools that direct users to additional content, or junk piles for all the stuff a site has to have but no one wants to look at. If you're designing for the former option, you will find that at some point a part of your footer will likely become a junk holder as well. Not to worry, though; like a license plate on a car, it is a necessary element that we simply have to learn to work with.

FUNCTIONAL FOOTERS

A very common approach is to take the footer region of a site and attempt to turn it into a critical navigation tool. (See page 054 for samples.) This actually makes really solid sense. Think about it this way: If a user has managed to make it to the bottom of the web page, we should provide them with pointers to additional content or key calls to action.

COMMON FOOTER ELEMENTS

Some elements we commonly find in footers include:

- Copyright information and links to legal stuff like privacy policies
- A repeat of a site's primary navigation
- A complete or partial sitemap
- Tertiary links to content very few people will want (like how to advertise on the site)

Many other things have been placed in footers, and there is no right or wrong answer. Just consider what makes your client's site and business tick. This will likely point you in the right direction for some element or content to include. (See page 055 for samples.)

FUNCTIONAL FOOTERS

1

Media Services | Creative | Social Media | Company | About AgencyDivision | Connect With Us

Television
Interactive
Media Testing
Getting Started

Television
Interactive
3D
Radio

Daily Deals
Facebook

Our Approach
Philosophy
Brand Strategy

About us
Team
News
Career

Intelligent and cost efficient
advertising solutions for
Brands & Direct Response
TV advertisers

Agency Division, Inc.,
13428 Maxella Ave, Suite 900,
Marina del Rey, CA 90292
T + 1 888 668 8327
F + 1 888 668 8327
Skype: agencydivision
info@agencydivision.com

AGENCY | DIVISION (888) ON-TV-FAST
+ 1 888 668 8327

http://agencydivision.com

2

I CONNECT SOCIALLY AT: ⓣ ⓣ ⓓ ⓕ ⓒ ⓘⓝ | SUBSCRIBE: ⓢ | CONTACT ME: ⓞ

http://ismaelburciaga.com

1 One popular approach for footers is to include a mini sitemap. This makes it easy for users to find the content they are looking for. This is so much better then simply ending the page with no additional information.

2 Many functional footers end up growing in size. This sample demonstrates that a compact footer can still be incredibly rich with options.

3 In stark contrast to the smaller sample, this monster footer is as decorative as it is informative.

3

www.pegasus-opera.net

054

COMMON FOOTER ELEMENTS

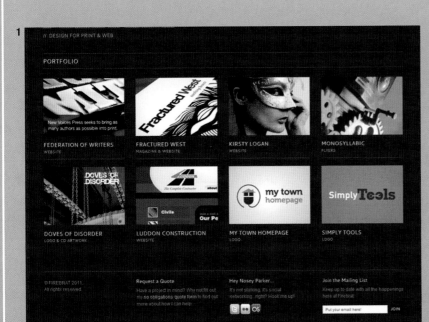

www.firebratstudio.com

1 This footer contains many of the most common elements, such as social media, copyright information, email sign up and other next-step options.

2 Some footers such as this not only contain the standard elements but also other bits, such as the series of brand names that help to promote the image and quality of the site.

3 Another really common approach is to include dynamic content, such as other relevant posts or recent comments. This encourages users to take another step instead of simply leaving the site.

www.funarisedie.com

www.smashapp.com

SOCIAL NETWORKING

Social networking has become a required element for many websites. Social media integration comes in a few typical formats. The first is in the form of simple links to the particular networks. In such cases, sites often have a cluster of icons that people can identify. This is definitely a situation in which we should leverage the well-known marks that identify a medium.

The second approach is to have a live feed of activity from the network. While it is relatively easy to integrate a feed into a site, it can, at times, come with limitations. For example, a Twitter feed is extremely easy to style into almost any format; while a Facebook widget installed on your site has less flexibility in layout and design. The key is just to tread carefully and research the network you're integrating with to ensure you have the required design flexibility.

I think the key with the social networking element of the web is to not assume that you need to incorporate it into every design in a totally custom way. These networks carry a lot of trust and brand recognition. Leverage this to encourage customers to engage you on these platforms. After all, a huge perk of putting social media to work is that people feel comfortable there; in a sense, you're on their turf. So again, consider using the default (or close to) styles these social media plug-ins come with.

PHOTO GALLERIES

There are two key approaches to putting photo galleries into a website. (See page 058 for samples.) The first is to make use of an off-the-shelf component for rendering a photo gallery. This type of tool is

SOCIAL NETWORKING

1

Tweeting...

Students! Don't forget, @chipkidd @kateconsumption and I are judging you. Submit! http://showusyourposterior.com
about 2 hours ago

You should follow Mig on Twitter here.

What I'm working on...

Show and tell on Dribbble.

Where I'll be...

Show & Tell Lecture Series via Skype
01/13/11 – Speaking – Portland, OR

American Ad Federation: North Dakota
01/18/11 – Speaking – Fargo, ND

7th Annual National Student Conference
04/01/11 – Speaking – Dallas, TX

AIGA Jacksonville Student Review
04/15/11 – Speaking – Jacksonville, FL

Weapons of Mass Creation Fest
06/11/11 – Speaking – Cleveland, OH

Columbus Society of Communicating Arts

http://migreyes.com

1 In this case the social media feed shows actual posts and updates, instead of simple links to the sites. While more complex, it is a great way to produce a stream of new content.

2 This slightly atypical link to social media increases the interest by providing the number of people currently subscribing.

3 Twitter is relatively easy to integrate into a site and often takes on a single-line approach such as the one found on this website.

2

2268 Followers
Why not follow us too!

1183 Subscribers
Subscribe to RSS | Email

http://blog.vtravelled.com

3

Teapot dice: RT @larosawines: Los dejamos con un excelente Blog sobre el Té http://www.teapot.cl //Gracias!! :)   Buscador   Ingresa tu búsqueda

www.teapot.cl

PHOTO GALLERIES

http://www.neuformat.com

http://hiddenriverevents.com

1 One of the more common approaches to a gallery is a grid view such as this. It works great as it allows users to quickly scan for content that interests them.

2 Sometimes text is not required for the thumbnail view of a gallery. Such is the case with this sample, where the images are the focus and truly speak for themselves.

3 This site is another example of a grid-based gallery. The subtle angles produce a layout that is rather distinct given that the web is naturally perfectly straight.

www.mccoy.co.uk

what their customers have come to expect. Is video a common factor? Perhaps social networking is more important than expected in the niche. Or maybe the technology is archaic and borderline painful to use.

The best place to start is by reviewing any web analytics the client might already have (based on current site traffic). If this is an option, be sure to get access. Analytics can tell you all sorts of things: Where does the majority of traffic come from (geographically speaking)? What web browsers are predominately used? Are mobile devices hitting the client's site? All of these things help you form a general idea of the target audience.

Put this data together and you have a formula for assessing the norms and expectations in the industry, as well as a clear view of the technological capabilities within the client's current audience. From there, you can make very strategic decisions in terms of your suggestions for the project. I can't lay out a plan for you in this area, though; it is so different in every case. But I find that by doing the two things listed here, obvious opportunities will present themselves.

GOALS AND OBJECTIVES

How can we pretend to understand a client's needs without setting some goals and objectives? Again, this borders on stating the obvious, but as you consider it more carefully, it's another planning element that is ignored more often than not.

By understanding the goals a client has, we simply have a better chance at succeeding. Just ask the client, "What do you want to accomplish with this new site?" You might get something as generic as "we want to attract more customers," but push for something deeper than that. *How* do they want to grow their business (because that is pretty much what everyone wants and what everyone says at first)? Do they want to grow their email marketing list? Do they want to start an email marketing list? Do they want to increase their sales leads to increase revenue? Do they need to better handle customer service issues so as to save on overhead costs? A fabulous question for you to ask your client at this point is, "What would make this project a success to you?" It is such digging that will give you a far better understanding of how to approach the project. Frankly, if you don't ask questions like this, you're just taking stabs in the dark—with your client footing the bill.

MAKE A SITEMAP

A crucial part of the planning process is the sitemap. A sitemap is nothing more than a plan for how all of the various pages of a site will be organized. This does not account for all the cross linking that might happen, but rather it focuses on the fundamental organizational structure of the site. Sitemaps can be a tremendous aid to everyone involved in a web project, yet they are all too often left out. Let's look at some of the benefits that come with them.

The benefits of creating a sitemap begin in the bidding process of a website. By taking the time to nail down all of the content that will be included in the site, as well as the critical elements of the site, you will find that everyone has a much clearer picture of the end product. First you will be able to far more accurately bid the work. By simply knowing what the site will contain, you can make a far more informed pricing decision. This leads to another huge upside to using a sitemap: Later on in the project, if the client says something fantastic because it saves lots of time and money. Even better, since we're using a pre-built component, we can allow the client to test drive it ahead of time to make sure they will like it.

The second approach is to custom-design a solution and build it from scratch. This can be a very expensive route to go (depending on the design), but depending on the needs of the project, it is definitely something to keep in mind as a possibility. If you find yourself going down this path, I would just challenge you to ask yourself a question: Does the custom gallery add anything to the site? If so, then perhaps the gallery is a critical element that deserves a custom-built solution. If not, then consider going with a more standard gallery that will save time and money.

The majority of projects will fall into the first bucket. Typically, photo galleries are nothing but a supporting content element. As such, it makes sense not to invest the time and money in a custom solution. This is where a really practical mind-set can help a lot. Pick a gallery that suits your needs well and get to know it. Then you will be able to easily design around it and know that it can very easily be implemented.

ROTATING BANNERS

Very similar to a photo gallery, the rotating banner is like a photo slide show in which we only see a single image at a time. (See page 061 for samples.) These have become a particularly popular component of home pages and work really well when limited to a few items. This sort of functionality is amazingly easy to implement thanks to many pre-built and very slick solutions.

The only thing to keep in mind here is that these are static images. This means that the user won't be able to interact with the images beyond a single click. This is one of those components that can please a lot of clients and cost next to nothing to implement.

CONTENT ROTATORS

Quite often the content rotator will get confused with the previously mentioned rotating banner. The big difference is that a content rotator contains a mix of HTML content beyond a series of images. (See page 062 for samples.) This has a few key implications. First, this means that each frame of the rotator must be coded to look right. This is not a huge deal but it takes a bit more time. Secondly, this means users can interact with the contents of the frame. This is by far the main reason to take this route instead of a static image.

STANDARD FORM CONTROLS

Form controls are the predominant way websites have to collect information from users. (See page 065 for samples.) They are also one of the absolute most troublesome HTML components to customize. As such, it is important for you to understand the obstacles web forms create, some ways to work around these limitations and generally what you have to work with.

If you ever need a reason to beat your head on the wall, try applying a custom design to form controls that look the same across all browsers. This is one of the most frustrating niches of front-end development. Several parts of these controls are simply unable to be styled with standard CSS. A perfect example is the drop-down select control. This standard form component contains an arrow on

ROTATING BANNERS

ziv meltzer
web & application design

First I'm a user, then a designer. I specialize in planning and designing websites and applications, for both desktop and mobile devices. And I write a blog. Interested? Feel free to contact me.

www.zivmeltzer.com

1 The large rotating banners on this site allow for full-size images instead of a click-for-details approach.

2 The photo slide show on this site not only communicates the site's purpose but also seeks to connect with its viewers through its most powerful medium, photography.

3 On sites like this, a rotating gallery can not only be informative but also decorative. As you will see here, the gallery does in fact direct users to relevant content, but it also adds a layer of style that brings the page to life.

http://alliance-for-africa.org/

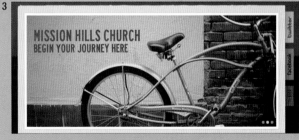

http://missionhillschurch.com

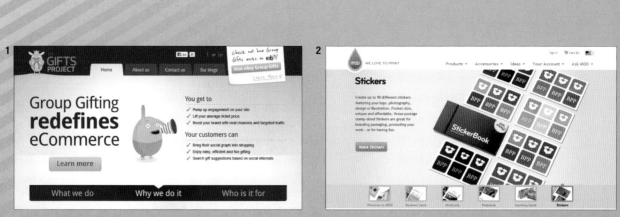

www.giftsproject.com

www.moo.com

1 This rotating HTML provides a step-by-step sales pitch for the site's services.

2 This rich HTML rotator allows the site to feature lots of content in a fixed amount of space.

3 The storytelling approach of this content rotator is a powerful tool in setting up a unique image for this agency.

www.integritystl.com

the right side that you simply can't target. Another great example is the file upload field (input type file). With this control, you will have amazing difficulty targeting the text box and button!

The problems with these controls stem from two key nuances. First, the diversity of default styles across browsers is staggering. And this is compounded by variations in operating systems producing different results. So, Firefox on Windows XP will render a drop-down control differently than Firefox on Windows Vista. This alone wouldn't be a tremendous problem, but the second problem makes this an exasperating issue. And that issue is the limitations in styling these controls with standard CSS. Many controls contain elements that you simply can't target and style with CSS. This means there are certain properties you're stuck with.

The difficulty associated with styling these controls is extremely important to keep in mind. If you don't tread carefully, you are likely to design something that either can't be built or would simply be very expensive to do so. Let's review some key input controls grouped by difficulty to work with.

FRIENDLY CONTROLS

There are a few controls that actually behave rather well. The text-box, text area and input button are the simplest controls. Fortunately, these are among the most commonly used. For example, in the standard email newsletter sign-up form, you have an input textbox and a button to submit the form. This combo is extremely flexible and should tolerate a wide range of styles. (See Figure 1 on page 065.)

DIFFICULT CONTROLS

The list of difficult controls is unfortunately a bit longer. The list includes: select drop-downs, select multiples, check boxes, radio buttons and file uploads.

With the select controls, you are simply blocked from styling the scrollbar and arrow controls in any consistent way with basic CSS. This will result in some serious frustration as you build forms for typical content. You can apply borders, backgrounds and padding to these controls. Depending on your design, you may need to carefully consider the production costs. (See Figure 2 on page 065.)

Check boxes and radio buttons have very similar limitations as well. You can control the text next to the items, as well as standard attributes like padding and margin. But if you want a custom check mark or unique box for either of these controls, you will need to think again. As you will see later in the chapter, there are some workarounds, but as far as basic CSS goes, you will not be able to do much with these controls. (See Figure 3 on page 065.)

Finally we come to the worst offender, the file input type. This is a control that allows you to select a file on your local machine to upload to a website. On the surface it looks simple in that it is made up of a textbox and a button. These two individual controls are easy to work with and are very flexible. But, the file upload control actually gets rendered from a single tag. And as a result you don't have the opportunity to target much of anything on these controls. In fact, you can do very little to change how they render. (See Figure 4 on page 065.)

STANDARD FORM CONTROLS

1 This sample demonstrates three standard HTML form controls: the textbox, text area and input button.

2 This sample demonstrates two standard HTML form controls: the drop-down input and select (or multiple select).

3 This sample demonstrates two standard HTML form controls: check boxes and radio buttons.

4 This sample demonstrates the standard HTML form control for uploading files to a web page.

5 This simple form is further condensed by using infield labels that place the label for the field inside the content area. This label automatically disappears as you click on and complete each form field.

6 Here is a super clean form that makes use of subtle rounded corners and gradients to provide a clear and beautifully designed form.

7 This form follows the more conventional layout of having labels above the field. The result is clearly larger, but equally easy to use.

1

Textbox

Textarea

This is an example of
HTML5 placeholder
text.

Input Button

2

Select drop-down

Options go here ▼

List select, or multiple select

Group 1
   Option 1 here
   Option 2 here
   Option 3 here
Group 2
   Option 1
   Option 2
   Option 3
Group 3
   Option 1

3

☐ Checkbox 1   ☐ Checkbox 2   ☐ Checkbox 3

◎ Radio 1   ◎ Radio 2   ◎ Radio 3

4

File upload

Browse...

5

SUGGEST AN INTERVIEWEE

Let me know who's career path you'd like to hear about and why and I'll do my best to arrange it.

Your name *

Your email *

Their name *

Why? *

SEND YOUR SUGGESTION

http://psftb.ryanhavoctaylor.com

6

Contattaci

nome e cognome

e-mail

richiedi informazioni / preventivo

◎ Accetto l'Informativa sulla privacy

RICHIEDI

www.moovents.com

7

Contact

Let's get it started, Contact us

Whether you need a simple Web site or something slightly more involved, it all starts here. Feel free to fill out the form below, or request a quote if you want something more specific. We check our inboxes obsessively, so expect to hear back from us soon.

Your Name (required)

Your Email (required)

Subject

Your Message

http://projekt19.com

FORMALIZE

http://formalize.me

Formalize is a fantastic tool in the battle for beautiful forms. If you just want your forms to look more consistent and have a clean and elegant starting point, then this tool will make your life much easier.

This JavaScript tool sets some new default styles for your standard form controls that give them all the same starting point for all browsers. This means your forms will auto-magically look more consistent and a lot cleaner. Until you experience the frustration of styling forms, you are not likely to recognize why this is an amazing tool.

FORM CONTROL REPLACEMENT

One radical approach to dealing with form controls is to replace them all together. This means that you are essentially hiding the default controls and rendering some other elements in their place. (See page 068 for examples.) These new elements are standard HTML controls that allow for total control and, when combined with a dash of

JavaScript, can be made to behave exactly like the original control did. Additionally, the new interface will set the hidden control to the selected values. In this way, the interface to the control is overhauled, while the actual control is posted to the server in the standard way.

I actually break this sort of control replacement into two categories, a basic and advanced version.

BASIC CONTROL REPLACEMENT

The most common place to begin with control replacement is the standard textbox and button controls. While these controls allow for a lot of customization, there are certain things you simply can't do with them. Take a look at Figure 1 on page 068 and you will see an example of two controls rendered with basic control replacement.

In this approach, the input control is rendered transparent by setting it to have blank borders and no background colors (or a background color to match the background). The custom frame with a hand-drawn border is produced by putting a background image on a container that wraps around the controls. In this way, you are guided where to click on the invisible (though click-able) form control. The button, on the other hand, is not invisible, but an image is simply applied as the background for the control instead of solid colors and CSS-based borders.

Basic control replacement is frequently used for textboxes, text areas and buttons. It does not require any JavaScript to work properly and facilitates extremely customized form controls. The problem you will face is if you need to style more difficult controls like select controls, radio buttons and check boxes to match. If so, then you will want to check out advanced control replacement.

FORM CONTROL REPLACEMENT

1 With some simple CSS, the standard textbox and button controls can get radically custom styles.

2 This sample shows how customized replaced form controls can be.

3 Total control replacement on the radio buttons and check boxes allows the designer to fully customize this stubborn form control.

2

Buttons

Buttons can do an action, display a menu, or both:

Enabled: Simple | Drop Down ▼ | Combo ▼ | ✓ Toggle

Disabled: Simple | Drop Down ▼ | Combo ▼ | ✓ Toggle

CheckBox

☑ unchecked ☑ checked ☐ disabled ☑ disabled and checked

Radio Buttons

○ news ◉ talk ○ weather (disabled)

http://dojotoolkit.org

1

Join our mailing list

Enter your email here   **Submit**

www.stopthevom.com

3

http://hellorent.com

4

ANTONY MORATO

Corporate ▼ | Collections ▼
My abbey road
Dualism
Day dreamers
Some days on stage
Lost translation
The denim news
Accessories

www.morato.it

5

LOCATION *

United States ▼
United States
Australia
United Kingdom
Netherlands
Other

www.awesomejs.com

4 While similar to a standard drop-down, this control has been totally replaced with custom tags to allow for a custom design.

5 This more radical variation on form control shows that total replacement allows for a much greater range of possibilities.

ADVANCED CONTROL REPLACEMENT

As I previously mentioned, advanced control replacement starts by hiding the standard form control all together. Then, JavaScript will inject custom HTML into the page. This new HTML will be styled with standard CSS and will allow for maximum flexibility with the look and feel of the control. This also means that the control can be more easily rendered the same across browsers and operating systems. Finally, the values selected in the new control are synchronized to the invisible control so that the form can function as it should.

In other words, this allows you total control over the end result. While this might sound like the fantastic solution I should have presented in the first place, you must approach with caution. This is a rather advanced method that can prove difficult to execute.

A fantastic example of this is Figure 3 on page 068. Here, we see some basic form control replacement on the search field and button. And we find some advanced control replacement as described here in the radio buttons and check boxes. You will even see a preview of the next section on invented form controls in the slider control.

UI CONTROLS WITH WIJMO

http://wijmo.com
There are a lot of options when it comes to control replacement, and I would like to highlight one in particular here as a great example and resource. Wijmo is a plug-in built around the jQuery library. This plug-in takes standard controls and totally

revamps them. The library also contains some invented plug-ins. And while the plug-in does have a commercial version, they do offer a free version that contains many valuable components.

A great example of this library at work can be seen here. The standard dropdown has been transformed into a totally custom date selector. You will also notice masked inputs and a custom numeric input field. If you're building applications or you need some super-stylish user interface controls, Wijmo is a great option.

FORMDECORATOR » OVERVIEW

Input

TextArea

Dropdown with Optgroups
D

CheckBox
checkbox1
☑ checkbox2
checkbox3
checkbox4

Radio
○ radio1
● radio2
○ radio3
○ radio4

Button
Submit

The Wijmo Form Decorator widgets (wijradio, wijcheckbox, wijdropdown, wijtextbox) are used to decorate a standard HTML form elements. The Form Decorator widgets allow any form element to be styled uniformly in any browser.

Date Input
8/9/2011

Masked Input
( ) -

Numeric Input
$250.00

INVENTED FORM CONTROLS

Sometimes you want to collect data from users in more content-specific ways. A classic example is an input control for a date value. It is much easier and more helpful to see a nice little pop-up calendar control.

Another common example is a slider control to allow users to select a range of values. In such cases, there are a number of tools that will allow you to create a totally new form control. (See page 072 for samples.)

You can custom-code your own controls, but standard practice on the web is to simply start with what others have done. And there are some tremendous tools available to do just that.

Three great places to start are:

- jQuery UI: An extension to the main jQuery library (http://jqueryui.com)

- YUI Library: Backed by Yahoo and filled with very advanced tools (http://developer.yahoo.com/yui)

- Dojo Toolkit: An awesome JavaScript library with lots of slick widgets (http://dojotoolkit.org/)

My biggest word of caution with inventing form controls is that they can be rather difficult to custom skin. While not impossible by any means, you will simply need to verify that it is something your development team is up for. If you base your designs closely around your client's library of choice, you will likely not be faced with opposition. For example, if your developers have made jQuery their library of choice, then by all means take a look at the jQuery UI library. These tools will be easy and comfortable for them to implement.

HTML5 will eventually have a huge impact on many of the most commonly invented controls. For example, sliders, date-input boxes, color pickers and spinboxes are all a part of this revised version of HTML. But don't get too excited; browser support is still spotty at best and it will take a long time for all of them to catch up. Even

INVENTED FORM CONTROLS

1
Budget: $4,800

Deadline: In three days

www.bjornenki.com

2
Basic Demo

This demo illustrates a basic implementation of Uploadify.

SELECT FILES

coucou.png (1.19MB)   ✕

Upload Files

www.uploadify.com

3
Noise Texture Generator

Opacity of your noise

Background Color

eb84d3

Dimensions of pattern

90   x   90

Your Sample Noise

Are you done, with your noise?   *Download now!*

www.noisetexturegenerator.com

4
widgets demos docs support forums blog purchase   SEARCH JOIN LOGIN

wijmo
UI for the web

GET WIJMO
Current Version 1.2.0

a complete kit of
UI for web developers

**Greetings earthlings, start
building a better web with Wijmo.**

Wijmo is a complete kit of over 30 UI widgets with everything from
interactive menus to rich charts. If you know jQuery, you know
Wijmo. Complete with documentation and professional support, every
widget is hand-crafted and includes premium themes.

wijmo

http://wijmo.com

1 A custom slider control enables the user to easily input valid data in an intuitive way.

2 This juiced-up version of the standard file upload tool is completely skin-able and is enhanced with extra functionality that makes it an invented control.

3 This simple application is much easier to use thanks to some non-standard form controls.

4 This suite of tools features a number of invented form controls that provide unique user interfaces.

worse, older browsers will never support these controls without some help. So for now, you will need to make use of work-arounds to ensure support across all user interfaces.

TABBED CONTENT

One common problem is having more content to present than the space will allow. A great solution to this is the standard tab control. (See page 074 for samples.) With this, each tab contains a bit of content. This allows the designer to pack lots of content into a confined space. In particular, you will frequently find these on home pages and product detail pages of e-commerce sites.

There is no need to code your own version of these controls either. As always, very smart people have already solved this problem in just about every way imaginable. I have made frequent use of the jQuery UI library's tab control (http://jqueryui.com/demos/tabs), but you can also find countless other solutions that don't require other libraries. One such example can be found here: http://htmlrockstars.com/blog/using-css-to-create-a-tabbed-content-area-no-js-required. You can also find countless plug-ins that work with popular frameworks like jQuery to create slick controls very easily. A fine example of this can be found here: http://net.tutsplus.com/tutorials/html-css-techniques/how-to-create-a-slick-tabbed-content-area.

ACCORDIONS

The accordion control is very similar to the tab control. Both of them allow the designer to accommodate large amounts of content, while

TABBED CONTENT

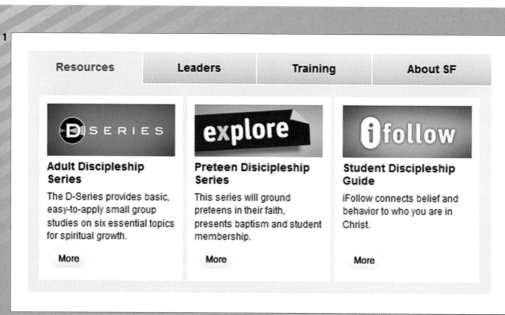

1

www.headhearthand.com

1 In this sample, the tab control allows the designer to keep critical content high up in the page, without overwhelming the user with too much information.

2 This tabbed content region prevents information overload by separating two very similar lists of content. It also allows the site owners to focus on a smaller set of options, which gives them more control over the user's experience.

2

www.cheshirescouts.org.uk

ACCORDIONS

1

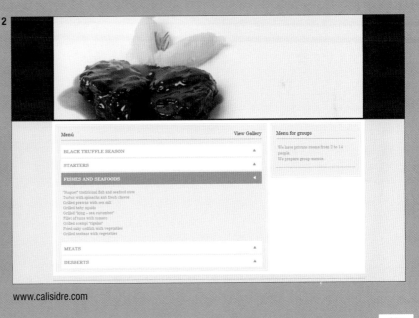

HOME   ABOUT   BLOG   CONTACT   PORTFOLIO

BOLD, Elegant Designs

New Designs

Design Services

Recent Works

Testimonials

www.ondezigns.com

1 This interesting example of the accordion control shows that it can make the content easy to sift through and prevents scrolling long lists.

2 In this accordion, a long list of content is easily condensed and made far more user friendly. It's a fantastic solution that easily consolidates the content.

2

www.calisidre.com

condensing it in a user-friendly way. The accordion control is often used for FAQs and other vertical lists that need to be minimized. One key attribute that typically defines the accordion control is longer text used to define the hidden region. While a tab control will be limited to one or two words, the accordion control might have an entire sentence leading the user into the content. (See page 075 for samples.)

Much like with tab controls, there are many great solutions already available for use. The jQuery UI library includes a flexible version, http://jqueryui.com/demos/accordion. Unlike the tab control, there are far fewer options available in terms of ready-to-go solutions. But, in contrast, the control is typically easier to implement and often requires fewer visual wrappers.

LIGHTBOX

A lightbox has become a frequently used approach in web design. This method uses a pseudo pop-up window to display a larger view of an image or additional content over the current contents of the page. So the content is not displayed in a new window, but instead through code injected into the page that appears to overlay and gray out the rest of the site.

There are two main reasons to use this approach. The first is that it allows you to show the user a larger detail version of an image, or additional content, without leaving the current page. This might make navigating through a series of items faster, allowing the user to quickly cycle through a number of items. Another benefit is that each

LIGHTBOX

1

www.locomotivecms.com

1 In this case, the lightbox allows the site to properly show off the features of the application without building pages full of unneeded descriptive content for each image.

2 This lightbox pop-up allows the user to quickly view each image without having to constantly return to the list view from another page.

3 In this sample, the pop-up acts as an interactive gallery that allows the user to cycle through the elements contained in the photo set.

2

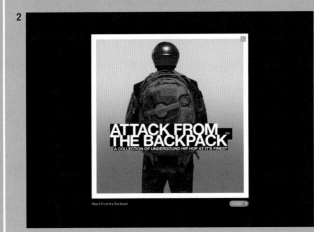

http://albumartcollection.com

3

www.ornina.es

bit of content doesn't require its own full page. This can make life a lot easier by minimizing the impact of everything getting a landing page. For example, you won't feel obligated to stuff all those pages with extra—and perhaps unnecessary—content.

VIDEO

Designing around video content has gotten a lot simpler than it used to be because it has become far easier to embed video into pages. There are a few important things to keep in mind with video. First is that you can't rotate the video in the browser. It must sit horizontally. Secondly, items overlapping the actual video might present a problem, though there are ways to work around that issue. (But you should be aware that it can cause interesting problems with older browsers.) This is one area to keep it simple. And be sure to consult with your developer if you want to push the envelope so you avoid creating expectations with your clients that you can't deliver on.

USEFUL VIDEO SERVICES

Vimeo
http://vimeo.com
This handy tool functions very similarly to YouTube but in a more designer-friendly environment. Its ability to customize the video player makes it an attractive option for hosting the video your site needs.

VIDEO

www.puttyhillmovie.com

1 Here, a bit more style has been applied to the framework of the video player to help it merge with the style of the site. Wrapping your video in this way is a safe and effective approach.

2 In this sample, the video is embedded into the page in the most obvious and usable of ways. It's a great example of keeping it simple and functional.

3 Here's another simple solution where the video flows with the content without causing any development issues whatsoever.

http://psftb.ryanhavoctaylor.com

http://radiantchurch.tv

Viddler
www.viddler.com
Viddler is a more commercial solution for those in need of greater control over their video hosting. This service allows you to isolate the hosting and delivery of your video content, which is especially useful if you have a large amount of video to share.

Flowplayer
http://flowplayer.org
If you want to embed video on your site and play it using a totally customized player, then Flowplayer is a premium option. Don't try building your own player when you can use this solution that does it better than you ever could.

FLASH

Despite all of the hype about CSS and JavaScript, Flash is still a viable component of the web. (See page 082 for samples.) Certainly the role of Flash in the marketplace has changed, but as with most things, it is always good to keep all of the options available in mind.

I believe that Flash went through a phase of overuse, as all technologies seem to. The trick is to look back on it all and understand how to properly employ the correct technology. Flash has settled into three main roles that we will review here.

FULL-FLASH SITES

There is absolutely still a marketplace for 100 percent Flash sites. It can be a great way to create a site focused on user experience instead of information. This type of site is often an effective solution for promotional work like movies and video games. The biggest thing to realize with a site like this is the key factors at work. (See Figures 1 and 2 on page 082.)

First, Flash work is inevitably more expensive to do. Every project I have ever worked on that was either all Flash or had a major Flash component ran into time problems. Flash work will suck up time like you have never seen. When doing this type of work, bid generously to cover yourself.

Secondly, Flash has some technical limitations. For starters, it won't work on the iPhone or iPad. So you will have to offer up alternative content, ignore the problem or take another approach.

Also, Flash content is not nearly as search-engine friendly. Yes, there are ways to try and get around this. But at the end of the day, it just isn't as simple as it is with straight HTML. Make sure you consider this as you plan a project of this nature.

Finally, content inside of Flash movies can just be harder to update. There are content management systems built for Flash. But you will not have nearly the experience you might with something like WordPress, where everything is made to be updated.

Don't get me wrong. I am not against Flash at all. Flash is an incredible tool that can build some absolutely stunning sites. To prove this point, check out FWA (www.theFWA.com). This site showcases all-Flash work that will melt your mind.

FLASH

www.mikimottes.com

www.booreiland.nl

www.pomine.it

1 Notice that the site is simple to use and doesn't require experimentation. The design and technology don't interfere with consuming the content.

2 This Flash site uses the technology to help communicate its content without detracting from the content or usability.

3 The animated bird in this site adds life and movement to an otherwise static site. It's a great use of Flash as a component of an overall site.

FLASH AS A FUNCTIONAL TOOL

One way Flash can really shine is to be used as a supportive tool. For example, Flash is still the most reliable way to embed video in a website. You have to produce some alternatives for mobile devices. Flash-based video is easy to implement and functions across all platforms and browsers. And when I say video, don't think of a standard movie you might start and stop. For example, in Figure 3 on page 082 there is a video clip of a bird seamlessly merged with the site.

Beyond this one bucket, you will find that at times Flash can simply do certain things that CSS can't. In particular, Flash can handle animation and complex interactions with a smoothness that plain old HTML never will. Flash as a functional tool is a fantastic approach, but this leads to my final thought on the topic.

FLASH AS A CATCH-ALL

I will caution you against excessive use (or abuse) of creativity. Oftentimes, designers get carried away with being "creative" and run wild trying to make everything unique and original. There is a time and place for everything, and such an approach can be appropriate. But, in most cases, this approach only hurts the client.

If your primary concern about a site is the transitions between content, the animation of elements or building some unique experience (that you have to explain) to promote the client, you need to seriously consider if you're taking the right approach. It has been my experience that there are designers only interested in creating what feels like an original work of art, breaking every norm and expectation on the web as though it was a plague to be battled.

I don't mean to rant against creatives by any means, but it is important to consider the client's needs and how you might help them achieve their goals. Most often you will find that this über-creative approach isn't going to work.

I place this in a section on Flash because one indicator that you're taking this approach is that everything you design can only be done in Flash. I have seen many scenarios where a designer creates something that can only be accomplished with Flash. If your client planned and budgeted for this, then no problem. But if you got there by trying to find the most creative solution to the problem, then perhaps you're taking the wrong approach. And it will likely lead to budget problems.

BANNER ADS

It is hard to think of banner ads as a design component. But many sites are only possible thanks to the advertisements that fund them. If you're designing a site on which banner ads will be a critical component, it is imperative that you carefully include them at the outset.

The first thing you will want to do is to dig into the technical specs for the ad service your site will be using. Some ad services will only offer a single size, while others focus on a small subset of the common sizes.

The real message here is to inform yourself prior to designing the ads into your site. And above all things, do not create ad units

BANNER ADS

1 This site has banner ads worked into its fundamental design's structure.

1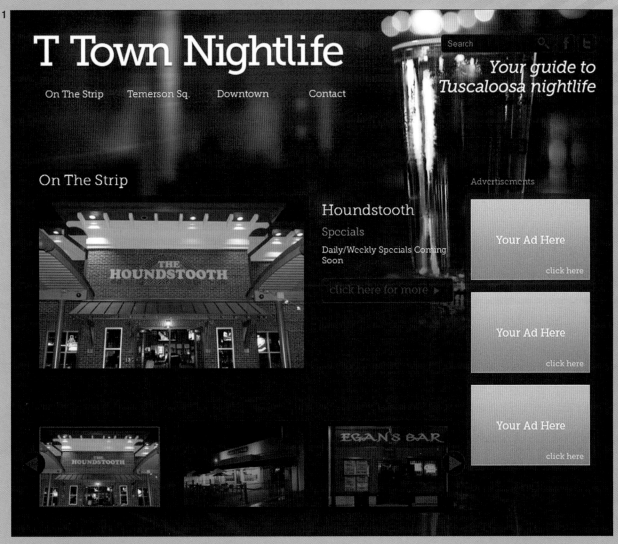

http://ttownnightlife.com/

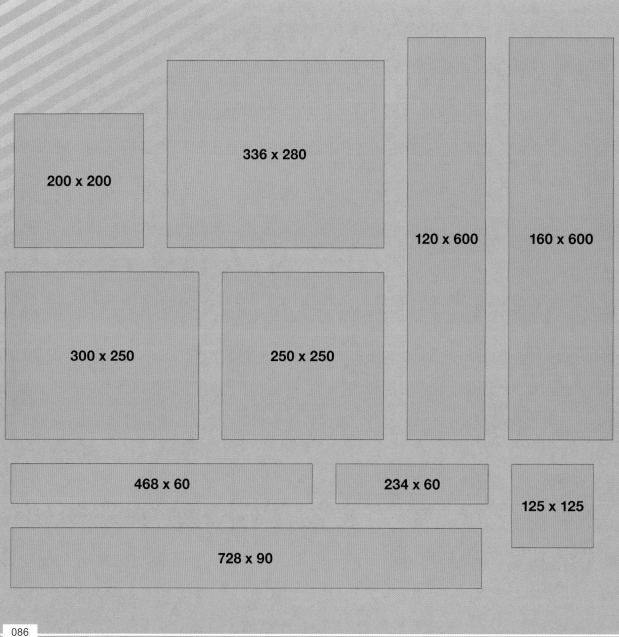

200 x 200

336 x 280

120 x 600

160 x 600

300 x 250

250 x 250

468 x 60

234 x 60

125 x 125

728 x 90

of a totally random size. If you invent a new size of ad units, every advertiser that ever wants to publish ads with you will have to create original banner ads. This barrier to entry will certainly reduce your sales. I actually made this mistake at one point and it killed ad sales until I corrected the problem.

STANDARD AD SIZES

The Interactive Advertising Bureau (IAB) has a standard set of ad unit sizes that we should always work from. You can review these sizes in depth here: www.iab.net/displayguidelines.

A great example of this at work is the spec sheet for working with Google Ads. If you plan to show Google Ads on your site, you can read up on the specs here: https://www.google.com/adsense/static/en/AdFormats.html.

See page 086 for the ten most common ad sizes to help you gauge the space they require.

THE EXCEPTION TO THE RULE

There are some exceptions to the rule when it comes to the typical ad unit sizes. A common trend in advertising is to see content publishers grouping together under a niche-specific umbrella.

A great example of this is The Deck (http://decknetwork.net). This network only offers up a single ad unit size, and it happens to be a custom size (120px × 90px). Another is Fusion Ads (https://fusionads.net). This network uses ads that are 130px × 100px. Both of these networks have broken this basic rule, and yet they still work.

The point for you as the designer is that you need to be informed of the specific needs at work on the site. Ask for information about what ad network will be used, then design the ideal sizes into your site. Planning ahead in this way will benefit your clients, save time in the future and help your clients increase profits more quickly.

CHAPTER 4

The Specs: Basic Design Limitations

All design work carries with it limitations. Some are intrinsic to the type of work being done. Others are imposed by the demands of the client, the budget available or even the time frame for the project. In this section, I would like to review some of the basic specifications of doing online work.

In print, every project typically comes with a basic set of parameters. For example, if you're designing a business card, chances are you will be designing something 3.5" × 2" and at 300dpi. Much in the same way, with the web, each web project will have a set of specs that drives the architecture of the site in a basic way. In addition, there are some commonly accepted limitations, as well as some fixed parameters, that apply to almost every project.

PLATFORMS AND SCREEN SIZES

For a long time, designing for the web did not extend beyond the desktop computer. Then the web slowly crept into the cell phone—a move that exploded with smartphones like the iPhone and BlackBerry.

Now, the Internet is extending to countless places like smartphones, tablets and even televisions.

As such, with each project we must consider the implications our design has on the various platforms it will be used on. The more you understand the various technologies available on which to access the web, the better you will be able to make wise choices when it comes to designing your projects.

With many projects, the very definition of the project will likely dictate the platform that is being targeted (typically the desktop). But even in such cases, you should be aware of the ways your project is likely to be used. I suggest starting with the analytics for the client's current site in order to examine the types of devices visiting the site.

If site analytics are limited or unavailable, you can also turn to some online resources to look at publicly available stats that provide solid baselines. W3Counter is a great resource for this: www.w3counter.com/globalstats.php.

Let's look at the most common platforms and the implications of each, with a particular focus on screen sizes.

DESKTOP COMPUTERS

The desktop is of course the baseline for most any website and accounts for the vast majority of web work. The biggest consideration when it comes to actually designing for the desktop is the physical size to design for. Again, we can turn to analytics to get an indicator of what size screens we should target. It is pretty well accepted that the smallest screen size that we need to accommodate for is a screen resolution of 1024px × 768px.

The trick to designing for a 1024px × 768px screen (or any screen size for that matter) is to remember that this is the full size of the screen. The actual amount of screen space available for your web page is smaller than this. This is due to all of the browser chrome (scrollbars, tool bars, menus, etc.) that occupies space on the user's screen. Typically, I suggest that designers design no wider then 1000px wide, and they should design with the expectation that a user will see at minimum 600px of height at one time.

I want to be really clear in that I am not saying you can only design sites to be 600px tall, but rather that this is the smallest expected size someone will see. The page will scroll vertically to adjust for however much content you put in. Consider home pages in particular. If you assume this 600px height, you can design the home page to ensure all critical elements fall into this space. This, of course, ensures that visitors will at least see the core content and action items you are providing them. This is essentially the digital equivalent to being "above the fold."

The really good news is that screen sizes continue to increase. Though 1024 × 768 is the baseline, the majority of users online now have screen sizes that exceed that. This makes online design more flexible and less like looking through a really small window. It does mean, however, that you have to design for a wider range of sizes than ever before.

Accommodate for the Fringe

An important thing to keep in mind when it comes to designing for the desktop is that while 1024 × 768 might be the smallest expected screen size, many people have their monitors set to much higher resolutions than that. With this in mind, many designers will add extra design elements to the background of the page. This way, if you have a larger screen you get to see something interesting. While not a required element of a design, it is a very nice extra touch to keep in mind.

So, what you can do is have a background to the site that is much larger than the smallest screen you might expect. This imagery will not be visible and it will not produce scrollbars for smaller screens, but it will be visible if the user's monitor is large enough.

MOBILE DEVELOPMENT

The mobile web is one of the hottest topics and an area of great uncertainty. Devices change constantly, and the market is exploding with a vast array of screen sizes and features. Developers are still settling into how to build for the current devices, much less the ones coming. And, of course, designers are still figuring out how to properly design around a platform with such specific technical limitations and boundaries. (See page 094 for samples.)

In many ways, mobile development is like the early web. There is a ton of experimentation with a lot of trial and error. The good news is that the mobile web is being built on a much more solid base than when the web started.

When it comes to mobile design, there are two fundamental approaches that greatly impact the designer.

Do Nothing

Yup, you can do absolutely nothing to target the mobile web. In fact, many people argue that you should serve up the exact same experience on mobile devices as on the desktop. After all, many devices can handle a standard website with ease. There are, of course, minor things to consider to ensure the mobile version works well. But in many cases you can get away with doing nothing.

Create a Mobile-Optimized Version

This ultimately means writing code to ensure a site renders ideally on a mobile device. In such cases we need to know what the basic parameters are to design around. In particular, what size should we design for? And to be clear, this is where things get really fuzzy.

One of the more notable examples of this is that iPhones started with a 320px × 480px screen to work with. However, with the release of the iPhone 4 Retina Display, the screen resolution doubled to 640 × 960. What does this mean for the designer? Well, unfortunately there is no clear answer. Because even if you design optimized for the iPhone, what do you do about the host of other devices out there?

The end result is that you will have to adapt your process to the skills and focus of your team. Up until the release of the new iPhone, one could design around a 320px × 480px screen rather safely. But with the new, higher-resolution screens, one should design a standard 320 × 480 version as well as a doubled up 640 × 960 version. Fortunately, there are easy ways to target the higher-resolution screens with higher-resolution graphics.

1 This single-column layout is standard for mobile web content. Notice how easy the streamlined page is to use and that the actionable buttons are really easy to find and touch.

2 Though it uses a horizontal navigation, this site is a single column that focuses on the content and less on the fancy containers.

3 In this case, almost everything becomes a button. Notice how extremely simple it is to touch and navigate to an article of interest.

1

Hallo!

GoodBytes is een **kleine webdesign studio** die **grote kwaliteit** aflevert, ook op uw mobiel toestel.

Over Ons	>
Diensten	>
Blog	>
Contact	>

mobiele versie - **normale versie**

www.goodbytes.be

2

WHO   WHAT   WORK   WHERE   BLOG   HOME

HELLO WORLD

Hola and thanks for stopping by.

Since we've only got your attention for a limited time, in a nutshell we:

Design and build websites from start to finish including Content Managed websites (CMS).

Optimise websites for smartphones such iPhones (including iPhone 4), Android phones and tablets.

www.talianadesign.com.au

www.webdesignerdepot.com

TABLETS

Tablets are nothing new, and yet, with the launch of the iPad, the market for them has exploded. Now there are countless devices coming out by various competitors, and the tablet is actually finding its place in the world. (Note that my commentary here is focused solely on creating websites that are optimized for the iPad and other tablets, and not on creating native apps to run on them.)

Let's start with the iPad, because frankly speaking, this is the primary candidate at this time. When it comes to considering the iPad, you have two main options.

Do Nothing

The first is to do nothing. The iPad has a screen size of 1024px × 768px, which is conveniently the commonly accepted smallest screen size for the desktop. This means that most sites that function well for the desktop computer will function well on the iPad.

Create an iPad-Optimized Version

The second option is to design a site specifically styled to work well on the iPad. In such situations, this is either the entire goal of the project or it is a huge add-on that the client will budget for. Either way, the project becomes a task all unto its own. I highly recommend that you don't make your first stab at this with a paid client project.

The biggest consideration in either case is the technology limitations. Most significantly, Flash technology does not run on iPads at this time. This is not the case for all devices, but it certainly is for the iPad. So forget the Flash and focus on the core technologies that power these sites: CSS3 and HTML5.

And, of course, the market is not limited to the iPad; many other devices are emerging. Some of the more notable ones are Android and BlackBerry based. By the time this book is published, though, there will no doubt be even more devices available. The portable device market is changing so fast you will be hard-pressed to keep up.

OTHER DEVICES: TVS, GOOGLE TV, ETC.

There are tons of new devices showing up that bring the web to new places. Most notable of these are Internet-ready TVs and TV-oriented devices like those that use Google TV. The real moral of the story is to realize that your site will likely be showing up on all sorts of devices and browsers, far beyond what your client might ever even comprehend. In many ways, there is almost nothing you can really do. There are just too many variables to accommodate for. Perhaps someday we will finally have the proverbial computer in the door of our refrigerators; if so, chances are it will be surfing the web.

WHERE TO GO FROM HERE

So, what do we do? Well, we embrace the best practices and do our best to make extremely functional websites. This will inevitably lead to sites that have a chance of functioning well across various platforms. Part of my hope here was to open your eyes to the ever-increasing range of platforms and the complexities they can present. Fortunately, the very definition of most projects will outline which aspects of all of this are even a concern. In many ways this should illustrate why it is so important to have a basic understanding of how things will ultimately work. This should also help us see why designing experimental interfaces and ignoring conventions are dangerous undertakings.

CONTENT MANAGEMENT SYSTEMS

A content management system (CMS) allows an individual or a team to easily manage the content of a website. Some of the core functions and purposes of a CMS include:

- Allow for multiple users to publish and manage content

- Implement workflow permissions and rules to ensure business rules are followed (like editorial reviews and such)

- Reduce repetitive tasks and automate basic features

Consider a blog built on WordPress, for example. The system allows just about anyone with a computer to write and publish content. No special technical skills are required and users need not know any HTML in order to do so successfully.

Before CMSes emerged and became a basic requirement for almost every website, content creators were at the mercy of site administrators who could code and add content. This presented obvious roadblocks to maintaining sites. Now, with many CMSes to pick from, a site's content can be collaborated on and managed in a much more efficient way.

HOSTED VS. INSTALLED

When selecting a CMS, you will find that there are literally countless options. They range from huge enterprise systems intended to handle multiple sites receiving millions of visitors all the way down to niche systems targeted at the local small business owner.

There are many ways to break down the variety of systems available, and for this section I want to first focus on the difference between hosted and installed systems. The main difference boils down to who is in charge of maintaining the actual CMS software. Keep in mind there is no right answer here; it is simply a matter of fulfilling the needs you have in the best way possible.

Installed (or Self-Hosted) Systems

With an installed system, you download the files needed to run the CMS and install it to a web host on your own. So, for example, if you are building a business site on WordPress, you would do the following:

1. Download the WordPress software.
2. Upload it to your server.
3. Run an install routine to set up the system.

Frankly, it is a fairly easy process, and you can typically have most any modern CMS up and running in no time. Let's focus on some of the key implications of running your own installed CMS:

- You are responsible for updates and maintenance.

- You are responsible for fixing any problems—like a hacker breaking in and messing things up.

- You must perform backups and recoveries as needed.

- You have the flexibility to add or do anything to the system you want.

- You can move the system to any web hosting service you choose.

- You have many free open-source systems to choose from.

- Your CMS can typically run on inexpensive web hosting.

Running your own installed CMS has many upsides to it, like less expensive hosting and oftentimes free software. So, for good reason, countless sites are running on exactly such a setup.

Hosted Systems

A hosted platform is one that is provided to its customers as a service. In such an environment, those who are building sites on these systems need not download or install any software. Typically you create an account and your site is automatically initiated and ready to go. Of course, you still have to design it and build everything, but the work of setting up the actual CMS software is already done for you.

Some things to keep in mind as you consider hosted systems:

- The software provider handles updates and maintenance of the actual software (not the website itself).

- The host is responsible for patching holes and preventing hacking.

- You are locked out from adding functionality or changing the way the system works.

- Many hosted systems are pre-loaded with extensive functionality.

- Hosted systems carry higher monthly fees.

Hosted platforms are a great alternative to downloading and installing your own CMS. Certainly most systems like this cost more per month, but they also require far less work to maintain and keep running. This, combined with what is oftentimes a very extensive feature set, makes hosted platforms an option worth considering.

ALL SHAPES AND SIZES

Content management systems come in all shapes and sizes. There are countless systems out there, some targeted at specific site types, some for small sites and still others made to run multimillion-dollar businesses. Let's dig through a few of the most critical system types available, as I believe such a perspective is important to ensure you select a system that matches your needs.

Blogs

Blogs come with a specific set of needs and there are many platforms intended to cater to them. Fundamentally these systems are intended to handle content that comes in a flow. While most will support static content, the real idea is to allow users to easily generate new blog posts that add to the flow of content. This makes things like content scheduling, tagging, RSS feeds and other fundamental blog features a core element. (See page 102 for samples.)

The reality is that most blogging engines are equally equipped to handle content far beyond blogging. However, if you have need of a blog, then of course the only route to take is to select a platform made to handle blogging.

Some key blogging platforms to consider:

WordPress
- Hosted: http://wordpress.com
- Self-hosted: http://wordpress.org

Some hosted platforms
- Tumblr: www.tumblr.com
- Posterous: https://posterous.com

Some self-hosted options
- MovableType: www.movabletype.org
- ExpressionEngine: http://expressionengine.com

I acknowledge that this list is extremely brief in terms of the quantity of options available to you. These are just some of the larger, more well-known ones.

Static Content

One of the most common site elements is standard or static content. (See page 104 for samples.) Let's say for example you're building a content site to be the online home for a food product. The content will likely be fairly static. But, this isn't to say that the site owners won't want to add new items from time to time. So, the content should be manageable via a CMS to ensure design integrity and ease of maintenance.

As you research a CMS to present this type of content, some of the most important features will include things like:

1

http://bbqwar.com

1 Here, the creative layout entices users to dig in and discover what the site has to offer. I also appreciate that it focuses on the writers more and the latest fresh meat less.

2 This more traditional blog layout doesn't quite fit the norms and demonstrates the flexibility we have. Note that it does do a remarkable job at being web friendly and effectively integrated into the blogging platform.

2

http://lauraburciaga.com

- Multi-user collaboration
- Editorial workflow features
- Content versions for backups

Then again, the most important features will really depend on the specifics of your project and your client's needs.

Here are some of the top contenders for managing what I refer to as standard content:

WordPress
- Hosted: http://wordpress.com
- Self-hosted: http://wordpress.org

Some hosted platforms
- Light CMS: www.lightcms.com
- Webvanta: www.webvanta.com

Some self-hosted options
- Joomla: www.joomla.org
- Drupal: http://drupal.org

E-Commerce

Selecting a CMS is a critical step in building any website. But when it comes to building an e-commerce site, the selection of the right CMS couldn't possibly be any more crucial. It is a choice that can either doom a project from the start or give it a chance to truly succeed. (See page 107 for samples.)

My suggestion is that you pay very close attention to your client, their needs, their processes and the features that will help them the most. Here are some important things to consider:

1 This static website consists of elements that can be updated but don't rely on constant change. The site is what it is and makes no effort to appear fresh or updated. This is not bad, mind you, and is simply one way to present your business online.

1

www.kymerastudio.com

- How many products do they need in the store?
- How does the system handle order processing?
- Does the platform integrate with shipping services?
- How do you go about generating shipping labels and packing slips?

These types of questions will serve you well when filtering down the vast array of options.

I also want to provide some starting points for researching platforms to use. I want to preface this with two things, though.

First, I am focusing on what I consider "smaller" systems. While these platforms can handle very large businesses with a large quantity of orders, the list does not include what would be considered enterprise-level systems. Frankly, if the project requires a system on that scale, then as the designer you are most likely not a part of the selection process, and the choice will probably be made before you even get involved!

Secondly, I want to encourage you to carefully consider a hosted platform. I have come across many sites that do millions of dollars a year in business and are run on hosted systems. Don't assume that a large business must be self-hosted. Keep your mind open to truly find the best solution for your client.

So, here are a few options to consider as you begin your research process.

Some hosted platforms
- Shopify: www.shopify.com
- Big Cartel: http://bigcartel.com

- Yahoo Stores: http://smallbusiness.yahoo.com/ecommerce
- ProStores: www.prostores.com
- Amazon Webstore: http://webstore.amazon.com

Some self-hosted options

- Magento: www.magentocommerce.com
- AspDotNetStorefront: www.aspdotnetstorefront.com

Blended Platforms

The truth is that most platforms are blended. Many systems can be made to behave like almost any other system. For example, three of the most popular free platforms (WordPress, Drupal and Joomla) can be extended in countless ways to fill almost any role imaginable. You can turn WordPress into an e-commerce store with the addition of a plug-in, for example.

In contrast, there are a number of platforms that set out to be complete solutions out of the box. Some of these will merge many feature sets into a single system to make overall maintenance and business operations easier. The only real downside is that these systems often have less optimal versions of various feature sets. For example, say the CMS includes an email marketing system. It will probably do the job, but it will never be as robust as a tool like Mail Chimp (http://mailchimp.com) or Campaign Monitor (www.campaignmonitor.com).

WHY YOU SHOULD LOVE CMS

Content management systems allow site owners to update their own content, something that has become a basic assumption for most site

E-COMMERCE

1 Sites such as this one, and countless other e-commerce sites, are built on popular platforms that accommodate for the majority of needs in terms of core functionality.

1

Home | About us | Our Blog | Contact us

You have **1 item** in your cart | View cart

et la mer

escape with inspired style

Search | Looking for something? | GO

FEVER
LONDON

AUTUMN FEVER
SHOWCASING SOON...

Shop et la mer

By size

XS S M L XL

Dresses
Tops
Bottoms
Basics
Jackets
Handbags
Gifts
Earrings
Necklaces
Bracelets
Handmade
Scarves & Belts
Brooches

My et la mer

Hello, Guest
Sign in or Register

We Recommend
Sizing
Gift Wrapping
Gift Vouchers

What's new instore?

stay in touch

When you sign up to receive the *et la mer* newsletter, we'll let you know about new items, sales and store promotions.

Your name

Your email

www.etlamer.com.au

107

owners. This oftentimes saves them money and keeps you out of the business of fixing punctuation and other minor things.

This is great for site owners, but why should designers care? The answer to this is simple. Most often site owners and content managers are not adept at web development, and quite often not skilled in the visual arts. This makes it almost a certainty that they will destroy the design with strange text styles or inappropriately sized images. This is where the CMS comes into play.

When implemented properly, a CMS can be set up to have multiple page layout templates (as you designed them). These templates serve as building blocks for your client to create new content. They also serve to isolate the structural elements from the content. The idea is to minimize the destruction site owners can inflict. This means that the CMS will help preserve your design's integrity. Notice I said "help"; it will never fully protect it. But at least the problems will be isolated and hopefully you can train your clients to leverage the system in the best way possible, all with the hope of maintaining the design's integrity.

CHAPTER 5

Designing for the Web

Now that we have a better view of the fundamental components available to us, we can dig into the actual design process. While I have no intention of telling you what specifically to design, there are some basic steps to ensure that the designs you produce will be properly prepared.

WHAT SOFTWARE SHOULD YOU USE?

One of the most basic of questions is, What software should you use to create web design comps? The answer is rather simple: Adobe Photoshop or Adobe Fireworks are your options. I am sure there are other choices some would argue for, but these are the two mainstream ones developers are used to working with. If you go some other route, you risk creating assets that won't carry forward for the client. So, do the world a favor and pick one of those.

I often get asked if Illustrator can be used to create web comps. The answer is that you technically can, but I would highly recommend you don't. Illustrator is vector based, but the web is pixel-based, so there is no reason to trouble yourself with the previews. Yes, Illustrator has an option to preview your creation as pixels instead of vector elements, which seems like a solution on the surface, though it is not. Inevitably the developer will want to open it up in Photoshop to slice it up, and things just never go smoothly from there. Changes are more difficult, and oftentimes the file is rendered with undesirable results. So again, follow the norms and stick with Photoshop or Fireworks!

SETTING UP YOUR DOCUMENT

When it comes to preparing your actual Photoshop file, there are numerous approaches, all of which are equally good. However, there are some key things to keep in mind that will help set you up for success.

DESIGN AT 72DPI

One of the first things to address is that when we design for the web, we should work at 72dpi. Don't set your Photoshop document to 300dpi; it will just cause your developers massive headaches later on. Instead, design at 72dpi and you will have an accurate view of what the design will look like in production.

To explain this further, let's consider what happens when we work at a higher dpi. Some designers want to work at 300dpi so they can use images of the website, or assets from it, in print form. If this is the case, feel free to generate high-resolution assets outside of your comp. But always produce the actual web design comp at 72dpi. If you happen to need a copy of it for print as well, then I recommend you mock it up after producing the comp at the lower dpi.

I have had situations where a design was produced at 300dpi, and every time I have tried to shrink that design, it turns into a nightmare. Consider it this way: 300 is not equally divisible by 72, so when you scale it down, everything will end up dithered and blurry. Let's pretend that we need to scale down to 75dpi, so 300 divided by 4 is 75. With this, every 4 pixels would become one. The chance of creating a design exactly 4 times the needed size is silly to even consider. So if you make a solid line 6px wide, it will scale down to 1.5px, which of course means it will be dithered.

The moral of the story is to stick to the natural 72dpi of the web. It is what developers are accustomed to using and it will lead to better results. On a most basic level, you want to have control over the design and try and prevent developers from messing with your design. Many developers are not sensitive to the nuances of design and can really destroy things. Certainly some developers are fantastic designers, but you should plan for the worst case, as design knowledge is not a requirement to be a developer.

Frankly, the issue of resolution is even a bit more confusing than all this. For even more information on the topic, check out the appendix "The Myth of DPI" on page 230.

PLAN YOUR DOCUMENT SIZE

Remember, if you're designing for a standard website (for desktop computers, not mobile devices), then you will be designing to fill a space no more than 1000px wide. I typically create a new document at 1200px wide by about 3000px tall. This way I have room to design background elements, and I have lots of room to extend the site vertically. While we might have up to 1000px to work with, I actually typically design to 960px wide at most (the next section on grids will explain why).

There is no specific size document that you should aim for. Just be sure to scale the document to accommodate the background. This again falls into the category of not leaving anything up to the developer to decide. Plan for the full view of the site in all directions, and scale it as needed.

USE A GRID

Grids have long been a fundamental part of the design process, and they are absolutely nothing new to the web. The basic usage of grids is well covered by the design community. The primary reason to revisit this topic as it applies to the web is to take note of technical advances on the web as it relates to grids, and how this impacts the designer.

In recent years there has been a huge movement in the web development community to rely on grid systems. These systems are code based, with a basic intention of streamlining the development process and allowing for easier implementation of grid systems in websites. You can certainly generate your own grid based on the size requirements of your design. But, if you want to design on top of these existing frameworks, you will have the added benefit of a rapid development and prototyping process. By embracing these systems, you will find that you have clear boundaries to work within … but inside of such boundaries come opportunities.

http://humblepied.com

www.vudumedia.com/

http://awwwards.com

1 The use of a grid on this site results in a basic alignment that provides stability and a sense of organization to the site.

2 Sites such as this make heavy use of a grid and are hard to imagine without it. In such cases the idea of a grid is not hard to accept.

3 Much more complex layouts such as this one are far harder to weave an overall grid into. However, as you can see here, the results can be extraordinary when you make the effort. Though this site is rich with content, the grid provides a layer of organization that prevents it from being overwhelming.

At the end of the day, these web-friendly grid systems are a way to streamline the design process and lower the cost of producing a site. The most popular option is the 960 Grid System (http://960.gs). Conveniently, this option offers some great templates to start your design in Photoshop or Fireworks. The great news is that if you follow the templates, your site will likely translate to code a bit easier. Your best bet is to pick a system and dig in.

POPULAR CSS GRID SYSTEMS

The 960 Grid System (http://960.gs) is arguably the most popular web-based grid system. There are tons of variations on the idea, but this one is the front-runner. Once you understand the concepts of working with this grid system, you will find others very manageable.

This system comes in two variants: twelve columns and sixteen columns. Personally, I have always preferred the twelve-column approach. While on the surface it might appear to offer fewer options, it has one fundamental advantage. The twelve-column layout can be evenly split into three or four columns of equal

width. How many sites have you seen with three equal-width buckets on their home page? Countless sites do this, so I have settled on the twelve-column option.

Less Framework (http://lessframework.com) is an interesting alternative to the 960 Grid System. While it is fundamentally a grid system, it is even more so a framework for accommodating for multiple screen sizes. This one package has basic structures optimized for desktop, tablets and smartphones. While it is more difficult to design around a changing layout, the benefits can be huge.

EMBRACE TRENDS

Trends can be an extremely touchy subject. For some, they are a great source of inspiration. For others, they contradict the fundamental basis of their creative thinking. And still, for others, they present an irresistible opportunity to copy other's work.

For many, the idea of working inside trends feels too creatively restrictive. Personally, this seems kind of silly. Especially considering artists have been trained for many centuries to imitate other artists as a part of their formal training. So what is it about trends that offends so many?

Well, what do trends really represent? Trends are nothing more than a common way of doing something. Trends tend to represent common stylistic approaches, as well as commonly accepted ways of doing things. If we ignore trends out of creative principle, we lose the opportunity to learn from what others are doing in our field. In the end, trends and best practices can be assessed and used in a multitude of ways.

So, for many, the notion of analyzing trends for valuable insights continues to be a tremendous asset. By learning how to work this option into your toolbox, you will open yourself up to a world of ideas and inspiration from the masters of your trade.

My suggestion is to embrace the notion of trends. Assess them for what they are and do everything you can to be familiar with what is becoming commonplace. This knowledge will only empower you to play into common expectations when appropriate, as well as to buck the trend and forge a new path when it makes sense. In the end, most design work is a combination of these things. The only situation in which pure creativity, void of trendy elements, is found is in the classroom.

LEVERAGING TRENDS AND STYLES EFFECTIVELY

Whether or not you object to the fundamental notion of trends, the real issue is how to effectively put them to work. The strategic question becomes: How do I leverage trends without plagiarizing? I propose a system for putting inspiration to work.

First, clearly plan and document what you need to build. This should include sitemaps and wireframes. This ensures that your focus is on solving the specific problems in your project. From there, begin looking at sources of inspiration that address the key issues involved in creating your design. For example, look at how others designed their navigation in similar cases, or how others dealt with something as critical and simple as flagging new products. In such cases, you're looking at specific details to be inspired, and not at the entire design with the intention of replicating it. From there, you adapt the inspiration and merge it into your final design. Ideally the final results should stand alone. Elements inspired by others will be so well merged into the final product that the notion of plagiarism will not be possible.

Note: A process for leveraging inspiration in your design is clearly outlined at length in my book *The Web Designer's Idea Book, Volume 2*.

PRINT VS. WEB

The notion of helping print designers transition to the web is nothing new. But I hope and suspect that this is a concept that will soon feel dated. I imagine the next generation of designers laughing at how old fashioned this sounds. But the reality is that we are still in an age of transition. Many designers have been trained with a focus on the printed form.

This new medium presents one fundamental challenge: Websites are firmly rooted in the technology that creates them, and these technologies set the boundaries designers and developers must operate within. The design lives and breathes on these technologies. For the printed book, the technology that created it is not the driving force of the medium; the final product is. But with the web, the underlying technology plays a continuous role in the way things are designed and built. As such, this shift has proven to be a bit challenging for many designers to embrace. I will do my best to communicate the critical elements required for such a transition here. Instead of focusing on helpful things that carry over from one medium to another, I prefer to focus on aspects of the web that make it unique from print. These are the critical concepts the designer must understand and cling to in order to be a successful web designer. For the most part, these concepts fundamentally contradict the way print design works.

FIXED-SIZE DESIGNS

The most obvious way to identify a design produced by someone bound by their print roots is when a design is based on a fixed-size layout. Before I go off the deep end, I want to clarify that I don't have anything against a fixed-size layout. But you will find that it will almost always lead to problems with fitting content and then changing that content over time.

The basic idea is that a design should not be locked in to a fixed or specific size. Typically designs will extend to accommodate the content. Most designs are locked in on horizontal width but are created to stretch vertically to accommodate the content. One of the most critical questions to ask when you're creating a design is what will happen when something changes. Websites are ever-changing, with new content, new pages and evolving needs. If your design is locked in to a very specific size, you will likely find that the actual needs of the site eventually break the layout.

Fixes will include pop-up windows for the content as well as in-line scrolling windows. Both are hard to use, break the continuity of the site and just don't make sense.

So, if you insist on a fixed-size layout, ensure you have good reason to do so. And even more so, ensure you have considered what will happen if the content grows or new items must be added. More often than not, a flexible design that can grow to fit the content is more suitable.

FIXED-SIZE DESIGNS

http://dansbodyservice.com

1 This design will easily expand to accommodate a wide variety of content, such as larger and smaller images and longer and shorter text. The only major restriction that sticks out is the limited space in the main navigation. Overall there is plenty of room for the page to expand to fit content.

2 This design is very rigid and provides a limited amount of space to work with. While not inherently bad, it does come with limitations that you should acknowledge if you're considering an approach like this.

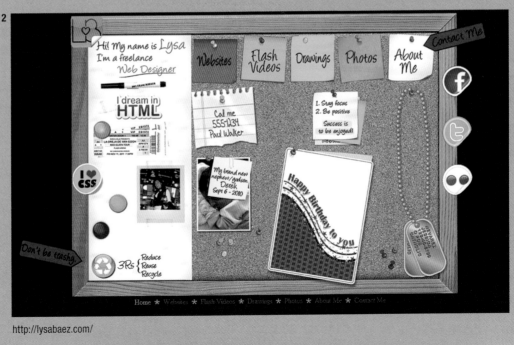

http://lysabaez.com/

As a rule of thumb, if your design relies on an absolutely specific horizontal and vertical size, step back and consider if it is the best long-term solution.

LIQUID DESIGN

While the vast majority of websites are built around the notion of stretching vertically to accommodate for the content, there is a smaller pool that flexes to fit the horizontal space available. While such sites are rare, they do demonstrate a difficult challenge. Designing something that can extend to any horizontal or vertical size requires the designer to carefully consider each design element. In such cases, consider each flourish and container to see if it could be easily extended in both directions. As a result, most sites that use this sort of approach are based on fundamentally simple design approaches, perhaps the most common of which is the full-screen background image.

While this approach might be a rarity, it is still an important approach to keep in mind. In some cases, simply having the page stretch to fill the entire space can be a useful tool. To say the least, the notion of a design stretching to fill the entire space available completely goes against the fixed-size nature of print work.

RESPONSIVE WEB DESIGN

While web design has traditionally been either fixed in size or fluid to fit the space available, a third option has become more and more commonplace. Responsive web design is an approach that seeks to

1

www.bnweiss.com

2

www.bnweiss.com

1 The layout of this page expands to fill the user's entire browser. This fluid effect is largely possible due to the very minimalist design.

2 The same site shown here at a smaller screen size simply fills the amount of space available.

ANOTHER EXAMPLE OF LIQUID DESIGN

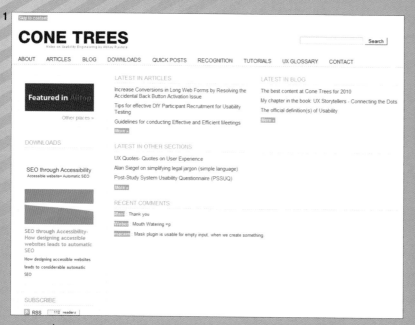

www.conetrees.com

www.conetrees.com

1 This site is very minimally designed, which again makes it an easy target for a fluid design.

2 The same site is shown here at a smaller size. Notice how the columns scale based on percentages rather than fixed pixel sizes.

adapt or respond to the environment of the user. This means adapting to screen size, platform and orientation. (See page 124 for samples.)

This approach is great in that it means users always get a site optimized for their platform. Even better, those operating the site need only produce the content for a single site. If running a separate mobile version of a site is out of the question, then this is a very viable option.

Core to this approach is a simple mechanism to determine which set of CSS should be applied to the site. Media queries are the magic component that makes this work. Traditionally media queries were used to target print style sheets to ensure a website printed properly. But with some simple extensions, you can easily target smartphones, tablets and desktops.

Since CSS allows total control over the physical layout, the use of a series of media queries allows the developer to load the appropriate styles. This means you can have a four-column layout on a normal desktop view, two-column view on tablets and a single column on smartphones.

This is a fantastic approach, but you should consider the implications. This means you will need to design your site to fit three to four different-sized screens. Even more complicated is that your site will need to be fluid inside of a small range around that size. There is really no way to begin to understand this without viewing it in action.

Let's consider a carefully selected example for this topic. This site was selected because the most common stylistic approach to responsive web design is to go with an extremely simple design. While this

RESPONSIVE WEB DESIGN

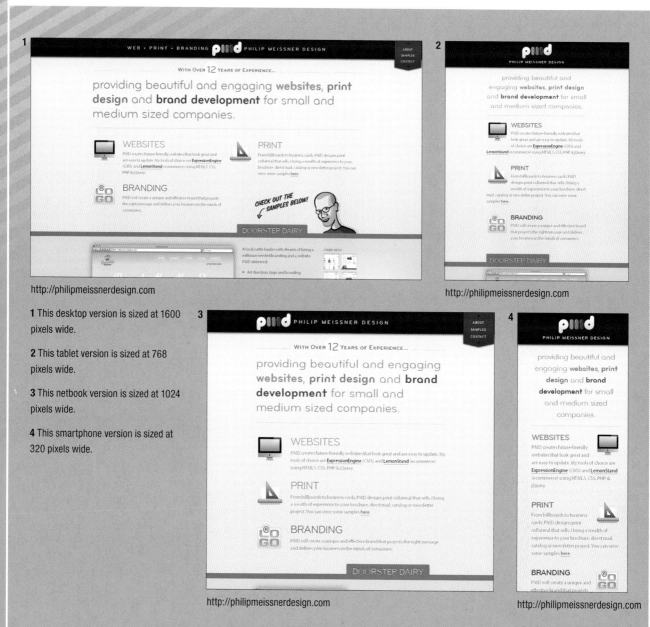

http://philipmeissnerdesign.com

http://philipmeissnerdesign.com

http://philipmeissnerdesign.com

http://philipmeissnerdesign.com

1 This desktop version is sized at 1600 pixels wide.

2 This tablet version is sized at 768 pixels wide.

3 This netbook version is sized at 1024 pixels wide.

4 This smartphone version is sized at 320 pixels wide.

sample does not include complicated containers for content, it does have a beautiful, graphic-driven design that shows responsive web design need not be boring.

As you can see in this sample on page 124, the designer had to plan for four different layouts of the same content. This means the amount of up-front work is far greater, but the end result is a site that functions smoothly across a wide range of platforms.

This technique is also still fairly undefined, as there are different opinions on how to split the various sizes up. As you will find if you dig into the resources in the sidebar, different tools take slightly different approaches.

RESPONSIVE CSS FRAMEWORKS

Media Queries
http://mediaqueri.es
This collection of sites is a fantastic inspiration source to kick off your responsive web design and a great place to see how this problem can be tackled in a wide range of ways.

Less Framework
http://lessframework.com
This CSS grid system is built to adapt to four key screen sizes. It is designer friendly and provides

a solid grid system to build on. This should help make the transition from design to code a lot easier.

320 and up
http://stuffandnonsense.co.uk/projects/320andup
Another great starting point for building responsive sites, this one takes a slightly different approach and starts from the small screen and works its way up.

Hardboiled CSS3 Media Queries
http://stuffandnonsense.co.uk/blog/about/hardboiled_css3_media_queries
If you want to write your own CSS and HTML, this indispensable resource has all of the media queries built and ready to go! No need to figure it out on your own; just use this.

STATIC VS. DYNAMIC

Perhaps the biggest contrast the web makes against the print world is the notion of dynamic content. While in the print world content is controlled going in and is often locked in from changes, the web is ever-changing. In fact, in many cases the content for a website will not even be generated or populated until after the site is built. While this is not the ideal situation, it is still extremely common. Such cases illustrate the importance of designing things that are dynamic in nature.

The more repeatable something is, the more likely the same code can be used to produce multiple items. For example, don't design

STATIC VS. DYNAMIC

1 Lists like this repeating series of links are easily set up as a dynamic set of content. Notice that the content varies, but the layout is 100 percent consistent. No funky exceptions to accommodate for.

2 A design such as this is obviously making use of elements suitable for dynamic content. But the large image that must be hand built and accommodated for represents an ongoing upkeep hurdle.

3 This design consists almost entirely of web-safe type. This means that pages can be easily added and updated with little effort required to maintain the navigation and other elements of the site.

www.burbujasmagazine.com

www.infinvision.com

www.blueluna.com

every single page of a site as though it is a free-standing poster. Instead, design them with dynamic content in mind. In this way, you create the framework for a page and then provide a number of content templates that can be used to populate the pages. By doing so, the design becomes far more dynamic and easy to extend. This saves time and money, as content can be quickly added to the site. If, in contrast, every single page requires custom designing, then the time to get something on the site is greater, and therefore, the cost is higher.

There are, of course, many situations where a fully customized design that is not extendable or dynamic in any way is more than okay. It is more about understanding the impact your design has, so you can make the proper choice for your client. A common scenario is to custom design something for a client looking for a low-budget option. It might not be too expensive to build, but it doesn't provide them with an extendable set of tools. Instead, they have to return for help for each new page they add. This situation creates a lower price up front but may create more ongoing costs for the client. Educating your clients on this is critical to creating clear expectations in the beginning of the process.

Fundamentally, the notion of a static design vs. a dynamic one is a matter of cost. The more dynamic and extendable a design is, the up-front costs will be greater while the ongoing maintenance will be less expensive. And while a site based on very static page layouts that are impossible to reuse can be extremely beautiful, they are more expensive over the long haul. Keep in mind that the majority of sites are best served by extendable designs.

DETERMINE CRITICAL PATHS

On almost any website, there are actions the site owners would like visitors to take, such as buying a product, placing a phone call, joining a mailing list or watching a video. These actions are considered critical points that businesses have identified as important steps in turning visitors into customers. Sometimes the conversion is clear, as in a visitor making an instant purchase. Other times, the benefits are the opportunity to sell to the person later, such as when a user joins a mailing list. (See page 130 for samples.)

Certainly, many printed materials have purposes that suggest a user do something. But on the web this process is even more critical. Even better, it is totally measurable. These actions are often mapped out along a series of critical paths. When you engage in the design of a site, focus on the core actions the owners would like to see occur. Use these as the driving force in how you lay out each page, how you interconnect the pages of the site and ultimately how you design the elements calling the user to some action. In the end, these actions are most likely the entire reason the client needs a website. Focus on maximizing this functionality, as this is how to impact the client's business the most.

PLACEMENT NORMS

Every industry has commonly accepted norms for how certain things should be laid out. It should come as no surprise that the web has some of its own. These norms are quite often totally ignored. I would caution you though; these norms bring with them some clear benefits.

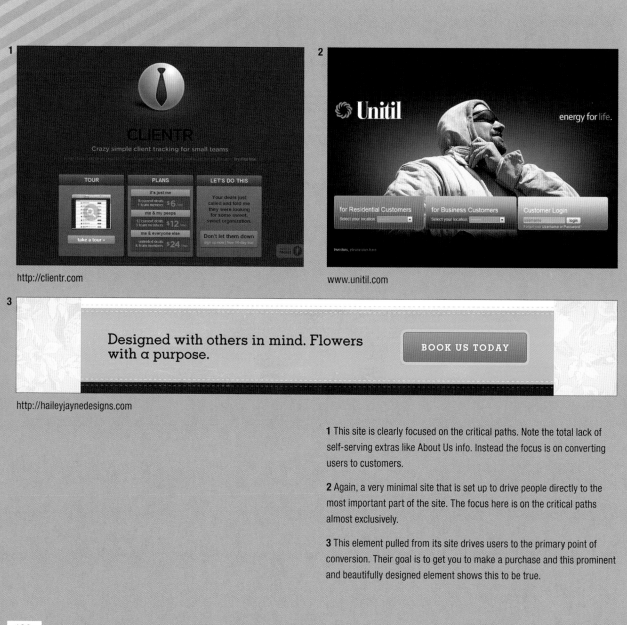

http://clientr.com

www.unitil.com

http://haileyjaynedesigns.com

1 This site is clearly focused on the critical paths. Note the total lack of self-serving extras like About Us info. Instead the focus is on converting users to customers.

2 Again, a very minimal site that is set up to drive people directly to the most important part of the site. The focus here is on the critical paths almost exclusively.

3 This element pulled from its site drives users to the primary point of conversion. Their goal is to get you to make a purchase and this prominent and beautifully designed element shows this to be true.

The first major benefit is that users have come to expect certain things to be in certain locations on websites. This means that if you want to make things easy on users, you can follow the norms and provide them what they expect. This can have a profound impact on customer usability.

The second bonus is that these norms have come about for good reasons. For example, while it might just seem like a common approach to put the main logo in the top left corner of a design, there is actually hard evidence to suggest that this is the best place for it (www.useit.com/alertbox/reading_pattern.html). In such a case, placing the logo in the top left ensures maximum exposure to the user.

What follows are four commonly accepted placement norms. Keep in mind that these are nothing more than strong suggestions. Every rule can be broken. But if you do want to break the rule, please carefully consider why and how it will impact the usability of your site.

Logo at Top Left

As I have already mentioned, users have come to expect that the main logo for a site will be in the top left. (See page 132 for samples.) This particular pattern is sometimes slightly altered, with the logo going in the top center. Either way, there is almost no reason to move it elsewhere, and a decision to do so should not be taken lightly.

Perhaps the biggest offense to this rule of thumb is the attempt to center the logo at the bottom of the page. This is also most often associated with a fixed-size design. Certainly you could argue it works just fine. But when you consider that you have no control over the height of the browser, you realize it is quite likely that a user is

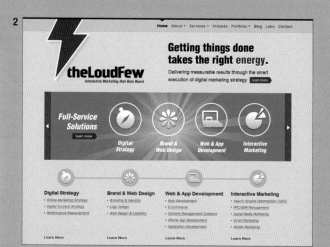

1

Join 44,623 websites using our real-time web stats

Realtime Web Analytics for Websites and Blogs

You shouldn't need training to figure out your web stats program. W3Counter is your free, hosted, easy-to-use website analytics solution for answering the key questions about your website: who's your audience, how they find your site, and what interests them.

www.w3counter.com

www.theloudfew.com

1 Logos are typically in the top left, but as this site demonstrates, there is some wiggle room.

2 The large logo in the top left could be mistaken for a design element and not the brand name; however, its location connects with our expectations and we automatically consider it the logo.

3 The logo in the top left corner of this site is directly in keeping with the most common practice.

www.papiniplast.com

unable to see or find your main branding. This can be disorienting to the user and cost you brand credit.

Login at Top Right

Many sites need to allow users to log in, and an industry norm has emerged for this simple feature. The most common place to find it is the top right corner of the page, which is one of the less prominent parts of a web page (at least based on physical location). (See page 134 for samples.) As such, it is a great place to put supporting elements, like login links, that users will go in search of. The top right corner is out of mind for the casual observer, but a user with intent can easily find it.

Main Navigation Across Top

When it comes to navigation, there are some standard practices that are nearly universally obeyed. The first of these is that the primary navigation for a website will appear horizontally in the header portion of the site. There are infinite possible arrangements in this space, but ultimately it is always in the header, and nearly always a horizontal band. (See page 135 for samples.)

Much like the logo, designers have opted for some strange arrangements of this critical element. By default, you should question anything but the standard approach. Forcing users to learn your way of navigation is a dangerous practice. Users have short attention spans and will abandon your site quickly, even if it is otherwise optimized for usability. As such, make life easy for your users and follow the convention.

LOGIN AT TOP RIGHT

www.thealbany.org.uk

www.advocate.ucoz.com/

1 Users have come to expect account access options in the top right, as seen here.

2 Login options are often grouped with creating an account and site search features, as found on this website.

3 While the terminology for this site's login information isn't standard, its placement is, and this makes up for any potential confusion.

4 Oftentimes you will find the actual login form in the top right, not just a link to log in.

www.infinvision.com

www.infinvision.com

http://joincollyde.com

www.fracturedwest.com

http://ncdthemes.com

1 This site's full-width navigation bar appears at the bottom edge of the page's header region. This is perhaps the most common location for primary navigation elements.

2 This site is another example of navigation being close to the top of the page, and quite often the full width of the site.

3 As always, there is room for some flexibility here; as this site demonstrates, the navigation can be a part of the header. In fact, it is a prominent design element of this site's header.

Submenus on Left

The second standard to navigation is that subnavigation for a section of a site will appear in a column to the left of the content. In close second place to this norm is putting it in a column to the right of the content. While the left side is more typical, it is also quite common to place it on the opposite side.

Again, many things have been attempted by designers. But this commonly accepted norm will serve your clients well in the majority of cases. This layout allows for the list of sub-items to grow without any problem. Sometimes subnavigation is made into a horizontal part of the header, and while this can work, it is risky because it limits the growth of the menu.

DESIGNING THE DETAILS

In the process of designing a site, there will be many aspects that are obvious to design for. These critical pages are the focus of the discussion with the client. But, as it turns out, there are lots of little extra bits that the designer can prepare for. And by planning ahead you maintain greater creative control over the outcome of the project.

Many of the elements featured below are going to be required to build a site, regardless of if you prepare for them or not. If you don't prepare for them, the developers programming the site will have one of two choices. The first option is to return to the designer and request the asset. This is the ideal option, but depending on the situation it might not be the route they go. Instead, many developers will give it a try to make something look nice. Even worse, they might be so blind to the design elements that they don't do anything to beautify the element.

1 The secondary navigation is on the left side of this site. This is the most common placement and the place users most often expect it to be.

2 This site has the navigation on the right side. It works well and puts the focus on the content a bit more. There is always room for variation; just keep in mind why you're doing things and make strategic decisions.

ENQUIRE NOW ▶

Features / benefits

✔ Downgauging possibilities
✔ High strength
✔ May be UV stabilised for outdoor storage
✔ Non fusion version available
✔ Range of colours

Typical applications

▶ Bottling plants
▶ Canning plants
▶ Bricks and blocks
▶ Building and construction
▶ Paper and board
▶ Polymers

www.ambassadorsforlife.org

www.brittontaco.co.uk

What follows are some of the most commonly neglected design elements that a proactive creative can prepare for. Being prepared saves time in the development process and increases the quality of a site. So dig in and polish up those assets!

BACKGROUNDS

When you're creating a design for a typical website and you have a layout that fits a standard 960px wide space, don't forget the background. Sure, your document might be 1000px wide so you have some of the background prepared. But if your design has anything more complicated than a solid color for a background, you need to prepare your design for how this will extend.

You should scale your document to whatever size is necessary to include the entire variation of the background. Let's say for example your background is a radial gradient that starts from the center of your design and goes out. Your file should extend until that gradient transitions into a solid color.

The goal is to prepare the file such that the developer will have a total view of what the background should look like. This will avoid having the developer generate the missing portion of the design.

HOW WILL THE PAGE STRETCH?

Depending on the fundamental style of a site, the question of how the design will stretch to accommodate changing content is oftentimes not dealt with. (See page 140 for samples.) In many cases, it will be abundantly obvious how the page should scale to fit any length of

BACKGROUNDS

http://the71s.com

1 Notice how the image-based background of this site fades to black. If you have a rich background such as this one, plan how it will transition on larger screens.

2 Complex backgrounds such as this one need to come with instructions for your developer, or else you will not likely get the expected results.

3 Again, notice how this complex background has faded to black.

http://lifetoday.org/

http://pulsehw.com

HOW WILL THE PAGE STRETCH?

www.cheshirescouts.org.uk

1 This page can easily stretch as needed, as the header, footer and sidebar are split and set up to slide up and down as needed.

2 This basic white container can stretch to fit any length of content.

3 This visually rich design has a simpler middle ground that easily grows to accommodate any length of content.

http://pilsenjuniortennis.org

http://www.bylerbarns.com

content (long or short). But at other times, it is far from obvious. If you are tempted to try and control the vertical height of a site rigidly, you should prepare yourself and the design for longer content.

Ideally you would make a variation on your design in which you literally stretch it and populate it with longer copy. This will illustrate exactly what you expect to happen. When doing so, be sure to not only use longer copy but also longer titles, more navigation options and basically more of anything the site owners might be inclined to add.

DESIGNING FORMS

Forms are perhaps the most difficult HTML element to style. As a result, most developers will leave them at their default state unless otherwise directed. Granted, some developers have some visual style, but you should never bank on it. Forms are also notorious for just looking awful unless you help them out.

Almost every site will require form controls at some point, but for many projects it can be easy to overlook these elements. It turns out these elements are quite often not included in the initial designs because the pages with forms are not the core focus of the project.

Following are two of the most important things to consider when preparing for a form layout.

Labeling the Form

Forms typically collect personal data that users can be very reluctant to give out. As such, it is wise to properly inform them of the exact purpose of the form.

Input Fields and Labels

Secondly, plan for how the input fields of the form will be laid out on the page and how the labels for these fields will be styled and oriented to the fields.

Forms are an element that when left to their defaults can look very awkward in a design. By properly preparing the design of these, the site can become seamless and much more effective.

FORM VALIDATION

In conjunction with forms comes a design element I have rarely seen accommodated for in the initial design assets: form validation. When a user is engaging a form on the site, there will likely be some form of validation going on. The code of the page will verify that the form has been properly completed. If not, an error of some sort will be presented. Design these errors ahead of time to ensure they flow smoothly with the site and the form controls.

There are four core approaches to validation to consider; your site may use any combination, or all of these.

Required Fields

All required fields should be indicated on a form. Most often this is done with an asterisk or other visual indicator.

Real-Time Validation

Some validation is done in real time as a user completes a form. This form of validation sets out to inform the user as quickly as possible of any problems with the data they have placed into a form.

INPUT FIELDS AND LABELS

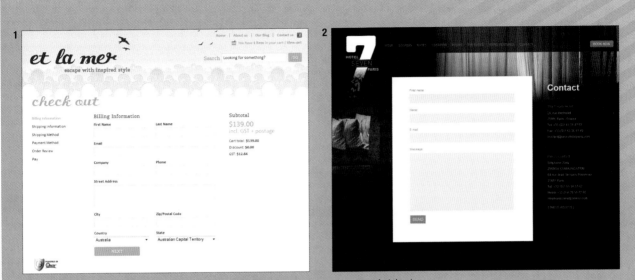

www.etlamer.com.au

www.sevenhotelparis.com

www.charlottesfurniture.com

1 While not the most elaborate of form designs, a beautiful form like this doesn't happen by accident.

2 Here's a clean and beautiful form that was well designed to fit into the site.

3 Here's a bold and distinct form that fits the style of the site and is easy to use.

A jQuery validation plug-in is a very nice example of how this can be accomplished.

Post-Back Validation

This form of validation happens after a user has posted a form to a site. Oftentimes the same style as the real-time validation is used, but another option is to group all of the errors into a single message.

Status Messages

Most often a user will need some sort of feedback after performing an action on your site, such as submitting a form. But there are many other events that might occur as well. Carefully consider your site and the actions users might take. With this in mind, plan for the messages the site will need to communicate to them. You will want to plan the content as well as the design for these elements. (See page 146 for samples.)

ON/OFF/HOVER LINK AND NAVIGATION STATES

While styling for various states of a link is indeed a rather basic thing to design for, you might be surprised just how often all of the details are overlooked. Be sure to include in your design the following states of any links in the page.

Normal Links

This is the default state of a link. It is not currently being hovered or clicked and is not pointing to a URL the user has previously visited. This is the link format that the majority of designers always cover.

POST-BACK VALIDATION

1 This site's validation is simple, but very clear and effective. The page simply grows in length to accommodate the extra content when an error appears.

2 The tooltip style validation errors on this site float next to the associated field and don't impact the flow of the page's content.

3 There are many ways to highlight errors, and this sample outlines the fields in red and presents a general error message.

http://getprofiting.com

www.carmodsaustralia.com.au

www.sparkpointstrategies.com

1

www.inflicted.nl

1 Confirmation messages can be more than text, as you can see in this sample.

2 This basic confirmation message lets the user know the message was sent. Notice it is presented in green, which indicates something positive. It would have been tempting to make it blue to fit the site, but instead the color green carries with it a subtle message.

2

www.paradox-labs.com

Visited Links

This is a link that is also not being hovered over or clicked but *has* been previously visited by the user.

Active State

An active link is one that is currently being clicked by the user. Most developers will replicate the hover state style for the active state if a design is not provided for them.

Hover State

Finally, the hover state is what the link looks like as the user mouses over it. (See page 148 for samples.) This state, along with the normal state, is the one most designers prepare for.

One of the details in this line of thinking that is frequently overlooked is that the various states of the navigation need to be planned for all of the regions of a website. For example, many sites have dark-on-light body copy but reversed-out footer elements. This means you need to plan for all of the various styles of links used throughout a page.

Also, keep in mind that you will not only want to provide these styles for standard links but also for any navigational elements like tabs.

BUTTON STATES

In a very similar fashion to links and navigation controls, you should be sure to design for various button states on a site. This might fall into the previously mentioned form controls you should accommodate

LINK HOVER STATE

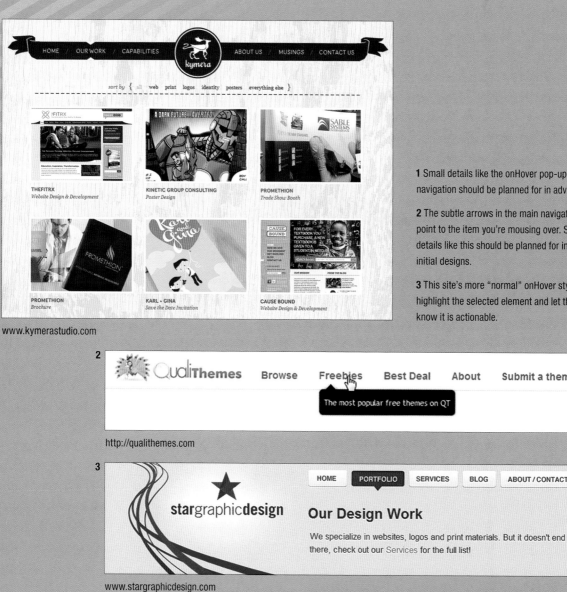

1 Small details like the onHover pop-up on the navigation should be planned for in advance.

2 The subtle arrows in the main navigation point to the item you're mousing over. Small details like this should be planned for in your initial designs.

3 This site's more "normal" onHover styles highlight the selected element and let the user know it is actionable.

www.kymerastudio.com

http://qualithemes.com

www.stargraphicdesign.com

for, but don't forget that these controls can be hovered and clicked as well. Ideally you should design for those states as a part of your standard design package.

The following sections outline the four states of buttons.

Default

This is, of course, the default state of a button waiting to be clicked. Most designers hit this one but miss the other options.

Hover

The hover state is when the user mouses over a button. (See page 150 for samples.) This state is helpful to indicate to the user that the button is an actionable item.

Click

Once the user clicks on the button, this is the visual indicator to them that they are clicking it. Providing this visual queue to the user can be helpful in minimizing the frustration of forms.

Disabled

The disabled state of a button is perhaps one of the least used, but it can be a very helpful option for the developers of your site. Seldom is this option designed for unless the designer has prepared for the validation process of the form.

Much like the various states of links, be sure to consider the various states of buttons used throughout a site. From pop-up login forms to search fields or newsletter sign-up forms—all of these buttons will eventually need a corresponding style.

BUTTON HOVER STATE

1 The search button shown is in its natural "off" position.

2 The button changes color when you mouse over it to indicate that you can click it to take action.

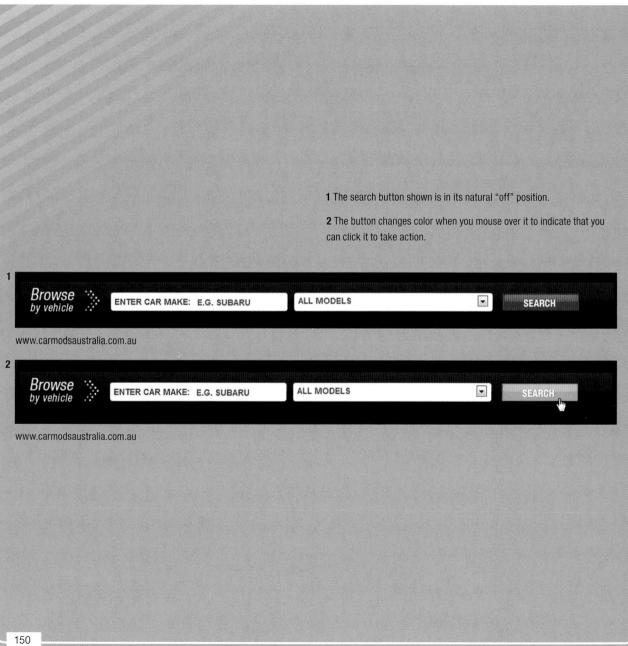

1

www.carmodsaustralia.com.au

2

www.carmodsaustralia.com.au

ALL BASIC HTML ELEMENTS

In some cases it can be easy to forget about defining styles for the standard HTML elements like paragraphs, headings and lists. (See page 152 for samples.) For example, many sites are so visually oriented that it is easy to forget that, at some point, someone will need to flow basic text into a page.

With this inevitable need in mind, be sure you provide a style guide for the core HTML elements used to mark up content. This would include:

- Paragraphs
- Ordered lists (lists with numbers)
- Unordered lists (lists with bullets)
- Heading sizes from largest to smallest in six sizes (e.g., h1 through h6)
- Tables for tabular data
- Type variants like bold and italics
- Form fields
- Images

Emails

One thing not many designers plan for is the emails sent from a website. (See page 153 for samples.) Such a basic element is easy to miss because it is not typically the core focus of a site. And yet, email is a powerful tool that can help promote and extend a site.

My suggestion is to carefully review the contents of a site at the planning stage to look for any emails that might be sent. Some of the most common examples include:

1 Sites such as this that lack blocks of standard copy can oftentimes neglect to accommodate for basic HTML elements like headings and paragraphs. Fortunately this is not the case with this beautiful site.

2 Pages like this demonstrate standard headings, lists and paragraphs that have been carefully planned for.

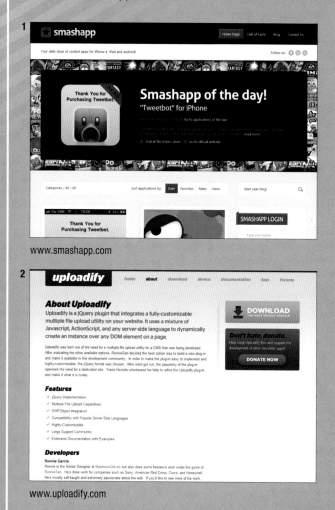

www.smashapp.com

www.uploadify.com

3

Heading 1

Heading 2

Heading 3

Heading 4

Heading 5

Heading 6

Some sample copy to demonstrate the styles

This is a standard paragraphy.Lorem ipsum dolor sit amet, consectetuer adipiscing elit. Aenean commodo ligula eget dolor. Aenean massa **strong**. Cum sociis natoque penatibus et magnis dis parturient montes, nascetur ridiculus mus. Donec quam felis, ultricies nec, pellentesque eu, pretium quis, sem. Nulla consequat massa quis enim. Donec pede justo, fringilla vel, aliquet nec, vulputate eget, arcu. In enim justo, rhoncus ut, imperdiet a, venenatis vitae, justo. Nullam dictum felis eu pede link mollis pretium. Integer tincidunt. Cras dapibus. Vivamus elementum semper nisi. Aenean vulputate eleifend tellus. Aenean leo ligula, porttitor eu, consequat vitae, eleifend ac, enim. Aliquam lorem ante, dapibus in, viverra quis, feugiat a, tellus. Phasellus viverra nulla ut metus varius laoreet. Quisque rutrum. Aenean imperdiet. Etiam ultricies nisi vel augue. Curabitur ullamcorper ultricies nisi.

Lorem ipsum dolor sit amet consectetuer adipiscing elit

Heading 2 is an important element

Lorem ipsum dolor sit amet, consectetuer adipiscing elit. Aenean commodo ligula eget dolor. Aenean massa. Cum sociis natoque penatibus et magnis dis parturient montes, nascetur ridiculus mus. Donec quam felis, ultricies nec, pellentesque eu, pretium quis, sem.

Finally a heading 3 to demo the style

Lorem ipsum dolor sit amet, consectetuer adipiscing elit. Aenean commodo ligula eget dolor. Aenean massa. Cum sociis natoque penatibus et magnis dis parturient montes, nascetur ridiculus mus. Donec quam felis, ultricies nec, pellentesque eu, pretium quis, sem.

- Lorem ipsum dolor sit amet consectetuer.
- Aenean commodo ligula eget dolor.
- Aenean massa cum sociis natoque penatibus.

Lorem ipsum dolor sit amet, consectetuer adipiscing elit. Aenean commodo ligula eget dolor. Aenean massa. Cum sociis natoque penatibus et magnis dis parturient montes, nascetur ridiculus mus. Donec quam felis, ultricies nec, pellentesque eu, pretium quis, sem.

Name: Enter your full name
Email: Enter your email addres

What's on your mind?

Message:

Send message

Lorem ipsum dolor sit amet, consectetuer adipiscing elit. Aenean commodo ligula eget dolor. Aenean massa. Cum sociis natoque penatibus et magnis dis parturient montes, nascetur ridiculus mus. Donec quam felis, ultricies nec, pellentesque eu, pretium quis, sem.

Lorem ipsum dolor sit amet, consectetuer adipiscing elit. Aenean commodo ligula eget dolor. Aenean massa. Cum sociis natoque penatibus et magnis dis parturient montes, nascetur ridiculus mus. Donec quam felis, ultricies nec, pellentesque eu, pretium quis, sem.

1

Operation Shower Network

CONGRATULATIONS!
YOU HAVE WON THE *NEWBIE* **BADGE** (See Your Badges)

Newbie
You created an account.

Stay involved with your network!
Earn more badges.

Login Now!

Unsubscribe mcneilp@gmail.com from this list
http://network.operationshower.org/unsubscribe.asp?email=mcneilp@gmail.com

http://network.operationshower.org/
Add us to your address book

Copyright (C) 2011 Operation Shower
Paid for by Operation Shower

http://network.operationshower.org

1 This sample email was sent by a website and was obviously planned out, not just thrown in by developers as they built the application.

- Mail list sign-up confirmation
- Site registration confirmation
- Form completion confirmation (like a contact form)
- Order verification after a purchase

Beyond this, if you really want to plan ahead and blow your client's and developer's minds, prepare a template for email marketing for the site. In this way, you provide them with a seamless transition from the site to the inbox and you maintain careful control over the branding of the site in its various forms.

DESIGN FOR ANIMATIONS

On a standard CSS and HTML site (without Flash), the notions of animations and transitions are so easy to overlook. In fact, if overlooked, they will oftentimes not even be accommodated at all. So, as the designer, if animations are a critical factor your best bet is to provide a sample of how this will work so that the end product matches.

Some of the most common places animations can crop up include:

- Tooltips: These are the little pop-ups that appear when a user mouses over some element.

- Image rotators: Home page slide shows are all the rage and offer a wide range of design options when it comes to transitions and styles.

- Lightboxes: Lightboxes can not only be styled in any way but can also be animated as they transition into the page.

DESIGN FOR ANIMATIONS

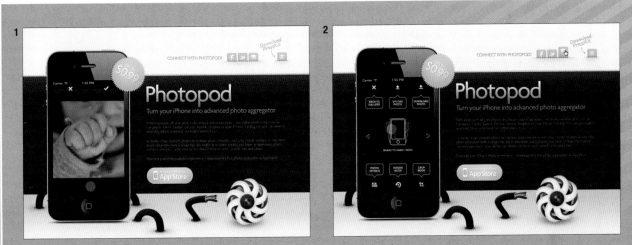

1 www.photopodapp.com

2 www.photopodapp.com

www.cybay.de

1 Note the current position and style of the social media links along the top of this site.

2 Here the transitioned state of the icon is shown.

3 In this design, the in-page animations are fundamental to the overall experience users have on the site.

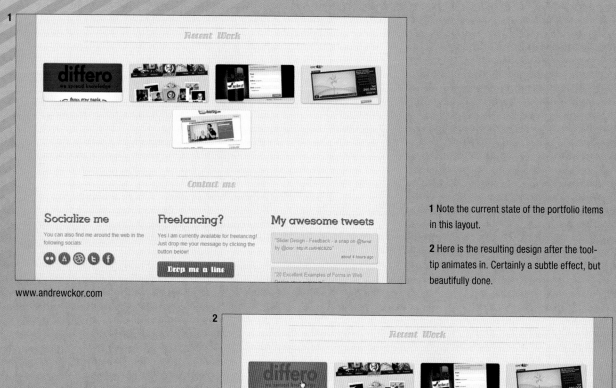

1 www.andrewckor.com

2 www.andrewckor.com

1 Note the current state of the portfolio items in this layout.

2 Here is the resulting design after the tool-tip animates in. Certainly a subtle effect, but beautifully done.

Interestingly, each of these additional animated elements carries with it a fundamental visual style that must be considered. By this I mean there are common approaches that are frequently used. While I can't document them all here, simply pay attention as you use the web and you will realize that you oftentimes know what to expect out of a certain feature. This is a good sign that you might want to follow the pattern to ensure your design is usable.

SITE TYPE EXTRAS

One of the most effective ways to take your designs to a new level is in the details. In this case, the details I am referring to are all of the little extras a site requires. There are many details that designers often neglect but that will be needed as the site is built.

For example, oftentimes designers will neglect to plan for how forms will be designed. And when the developers build out your site, a basic contact form is a likely necessity. The end result is often that the developer will build out a form with no design to work from. The results can range from awful to okay. But who wants an "okay" design? This is just another opportunity for the designer to plan ahead and design the site.

There are countless possibilities in terms of extras. Some are a given and very common, while others are specific to the site and project you're working on. Most often you can discover many of these elements as you work on the design, assuming you're looking for them. Simply ask yourself questions like:

- What happens when I mouse over x, y or z?
- Have I planned for all the types of content the site will contain?

- Have I planned all of the basic text sizes and elements?
- Do I have a design that accommodates for every page on the sitemap?

A friend of mine refers to this as "awesome sauce." When you come across designers who plan for all of the extras, all the little details, the end result is almost always better. This awesome sauce is a simple way to push your designs forward; it just takes extra time.

Let's run through a few key site types and consider some site extras they might need. I can't, and won't, cover every possibility, but this should be enough to get you thinking about your own projects.

APPLICATIONS

One particular type of site that tends to have tons of extras is the web-based application. If you are new to this type of work, then I guarantee accounting for the extras will make a world of difference.

On a most basic level consider how all the different types of data will be shown in the application. The simplest way to extend this is to plan the design in case no data is present, something that is perhaps far less frequently considered.

Here are some other things to keep in mind in order to get you thinking.

Forms Forms Forms

One thing that web applications are rich with is forms. You will likely find that the application's primary functions revolve around forms. As such you should very carefully plan for the types of forms your app will need.

FORMS FORMS FORMS

1

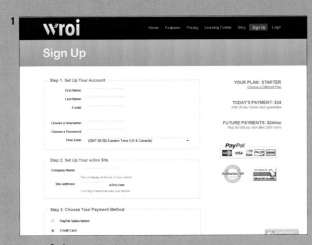

www.w3roi.com

1 Forms such as these are oftentimes an application's primary form of user interaction. Here, it is refreshing to see that they were carefully planned for and worked into the site's design.

2 This site's forms are customized mostly with fancy containers. This minimizes cross-browser issues and makes the site easier to maintain.

2

- My Profile / Sites
- Add Site Profile
- Profile Settings
- Billing Settings
- Change Password
- Upgrade
- Payment History
- Affiliate Setup
- Affiliate Summary

Edit a Site Profile

Site profiles store your detection history, mobile analytics and redirection rules.

Site Name Mobile sniffing

Site Address (URL) domain.com

Redirection Rules

Create rules to redirect mobile visitors from a normal site, to a mobile site. The most basic redirection is one rule that redirects all mobile visitors. See the screencast (video) for examples.

If you're redirecting via API Kit then you can skip this section. Click Add New Rule to get started.

Smart Redirection ✓

Handheld	✗ →

Tablet	✗ ↓

Rule Name
Tablet
Match ANY of these conditions
Is Tablet? ▾ Is ▾ true ✗
Match ALL of these conditions
Redirect to this URL
domain.com/tablet

Desktop	✗ →

ADD NEW RULE **CANCEL** **SAVE**

www.handsetdetection.com

Here are some extra bits to plan for with application forms:

- Tooltips to provide in-line help when you mouse over elements

- Validation styles as form fields are checked for acceptable data (For example, if you put an invalid date into a date field, what will that look like?)

- Design for the form confirmation page

Form field states:

- Normal
- Selected (the current field with the cursor)
- Disabled
- Errors (fields with invalid data)
- Optional fields
- Mandatory fields
- Reports of data
- Graphs and charts

Messages: Error, Updates, Success

Another critical element is the presentation of status messages to the user. What will error messages look like? What if a user successfully does something; what will that look like? What if there is some data that might be invalid; what would a warning message look like?

Think through all the messages that your site will need to communicate to users and then plan for them. Your developer will love you for it, and the end result will be that much better!

MESSAGES: ERROR, UPDATES, SUCCESS

1 This simple confirmation message tells the user the action was successful. Notice how sharply it contrasts with the design to ensure it is visible.

2 This error message uses red to indicate a problem.

1

Your site profile has been updated

www.handsetdetection.com

2

Comments

No comment added yet

Leave a Comment

Whoops! Please check you typed a valid email address and have filled in fields marked with a ' * '.

Name:*

Email:*

URL:

Comments:*

> Submit

Bristol Usability Group:
http://ning.it/f7eQRF #
2011/03/22

A good digital user
experience: http://t.co
/joZSV9 Nice article. #
2011/03/21

Interesting article about the
need for greater
collaboration between UX
and marketing to design for
holistic CX: http://bit.ly
/gBh6ZI # 2011/03/08

Follow us on twitter

net
+ Add sexy
fonts to
your site
>Power up
your website
with APIs

View article

net
+ Create
great viral
campaigns
>Unleash
the hottest
design tips!

www.superuserstudio.com

E-COMMERCE

Another type of site that has countless details that are frequently overlooked is e-commerce. Here are but a few elements to think about beyond the obvious pages of such a site:

- Emails that the site sends (order receipts, new accounts, etc.)
- The checkout process
- The shopping cart
- Checkout and payment forms
- Order confirmation page
- "My account" sections
- Account details and settings
- Order history
- Customer service inquiries

Again, there are countless tiny elements that will literally transform your design if you plan for them. I hope that this section really gets you thinking about your design. One of the best ways to identify the elements you're missing is to look at a site that has already been implemented based on your design. Do you see lots of elements in the final product that you did not design? If so, those are the details that you could have thought through and designed.

PREPARATION FOR DEVELOPMENT

Unless you happen to be coding your own design, chances are you're going to have to hand your design files over to someone else. And not surprisingly, there is a lot you can do to positively impact the process.

You will find that the cleaner your files are, the smoother things will go. Some clear-cut benefits of clean files include:

- Reduced coding time
- More accurate translation from design to reality

It really just comes down to common courtesy. Much like wiping your sweat off the equipment at the gym, we should really be delivering clean, well-organized files to the developers working on our projects. Doing so will build a stronger relationship between the two areas. And this will lead to a greater opportunity for you to learn what happens to your design after you toss it over the fence. Even more so, it will make you more valuable as you help save your developers time.

ORGANIZATION IS KING

It really just comes down to being organized. Photoshop and Fireworks provide basic tools for organizing your files. They also have simple-to-use systems for adding notes to a design file.

Use Folders

The biggest thing you can do is to make heavy use of folders. Break your design into clear modules and organize them into folders. A very helpful breakdown will include background, header, footer, left column and content regions.

Don't forget that you can have folders inside of folders. So that left column bucket should have a series of sub-buckets for each module inside of it. Ultimately the developer should be able to quickly turn portions of your design on and off without any trouble in order to isolate individual elements. A developer has to do this in order to slice the design up for the web.

As you create your design, it is likely you will need to shuffle things around during the process. If you find that you can easily grab a navigation menu or other element from one folder and quickly move the entire element, then you are probably on track.

Be Consistent

Consistency is very important when organizing your files. A perfect example is when you are defining the hover states for a button. Develop a standard way of organizing the assets to create the various states of elements that have interactive properties. Clearly label your folders and organize them the same way every time. Otherwise, you may end up confusing the developer who may inadvertently reverse your on/off states.

Name Layers

There is nothing quite as annoying as a humongous Photoshop file with no folders and no layers named. This sort of thing leads to a lot of guesswork, which really means your design will not be accurately translated to code. Name your layers and layer groups whenever possible. Layer groups should always be labeled, and sometimes you can skip naming layers inside a folder.

A good rule of thumb is to label anything you find yourself hunting for. You're the one creating the document, and if you have trouble finding it, your developer will as well. In fact, your developer may manage to completely neglect elements as a result of poor naming.

Add Notes When Necessary

Perhaps the least-used organizing tool inside Photoshop is its ability to add notes. You can literally add a virtual note right on top of your document. But in all my years working on the web, I can count on one hand the number of designs I have worked with that made use of this tool.

Your organization might communicate this information other ways. But this handy tool can really help you keep track of extra details that might otherwise get overlooked. If there is any chance you will not get to work directly with the developer on the implementation of the design, then it is in your best interest to add comments whenever appropriate.

BE AVAILABLE

Even though you might attempt to plan for every last detail of a site, you will most likely miss something. This is why it is important to build a solid relationship between the design and development teams. As the designer, you should make yourself available to the developers. Hopefully they will feel comfortable coming to you as they run across things they need a design for.

From the developer's side, it can be really frustrating when a designer drops the comps in your lap and disappears onto another project. Your design work is not done until the site is live. So build time into your project plans to accommodate for some extra details as they come up.

As a designer, if you stay involved after the fact, it can make all the difference. Don't consider yourself done when you hand over the comps. This simple tactic can be the difference between an okay site and an amazing one.

ORGANIZATION IS KING

1 This design is clearly broken down into layer groups to help the developer on the project find the assets that go together.

2 Here you can see how layer groups and layer color coding have been used to enhance the organization of the file.

3 With a well-organized file, it is easy to isolate single elements of the design. This makes it easy for the developers to slice the image up and replicate it in CSS and HTML.

http://authenticjobs.com

http://authenticjobs.com

http://authenticjobs.com

CHAPTER 6

Production Considerations

When your design is complete, organized and client-approved, you will be ready to hand it over to the developers of your site. In some cases this might be you, the designer. In most situations, you will have one or more developers working on the site who handle conversion from concept to a live site. The diversity of approaches is wide, but most of the steps and needs are the same.

One point of diversity is in the way work is split up. For example, a common trend is to have designers producing the starting CSS, HTML and JavaScript for a site that is handed over to the developers. For the sake of this book, I am not concerned with how the work is divided, but more with the various things that have to happen along the way. I am going to assume that you are new to the front-end work and, as a result, need to be introduced to the most critical factors. Let's review some of the most important things for you to keep in mind as you design and plan for this part of the project.

FIRST, BE FINISHED

One of the biggest mistakes you will want to avoid at this point is making the transition to production before you're done designing. Certainly every design could use more time, so you have to decide to cut things off eventually. But don't go to production thinking we will figure out x or y later. Or with the attitude that "Oh, we can change that later. It's the web, after all: it's easy to change."

These approaches will only have negative impacts later on. If a problem is too difficult to push through now, it will be just as hard later on. And if you have the developers make something now only to change it later, you will waste time. Though the web can always change, it takes far longer to rearrange a web page than it does a Photoshop file. For example, every time you change things during production, the developers will have to retest everything across browsers and platforms and fix any problems. It is far more costly to fix things in code instead of at design time.

CUTS (XHTML/CSS)

One of the first stages your design will go through is a process often referred to as "cuts." During this process, your design will be sliced into any number of individual images. These images are applied to the HTML of the page using CSS. In this way, your design is literally cut up and reassembled as HTML, CSS and multiple image files.

At this stage the developer will also bring various interactive elements to life. This is when the code for link states, button states, forms, drop-down menus and any special plug-ins your site might make use of are created.

As your design is sliced into various pieces, it will be compressed and exported in a web-appropriate file. Appropriate file formats include GIF, JPEG and PNG. A final site will typically contain a mix of all three of these formats. Here is a quick overview of the various formats.

GIF

Because a GIF file cannot have more than 256 colors in it, this type of image is ideal for files that have a small number of colors. It's also great for structural images that are based on solid colors. Gradients and photographs will not work well with this format. GIFs can contain multiple frames that can be used to create animations—a feature that has been used for both good and evil.

JPEG

The JPEG file format is ideal for photographs. The file type uses a compression algorithm that makes it a poor choice for images with text or large blocks of solid color.

PNG

The PNG is very similar to the GIF (though it supports far more colors). Its biggest feature that makes it a critical part of web development is its support for alpha transparency. This means that it can contain pixels with varying degrees of transparency. This varying transparency is the foundation of many sites.

THE SEMANTIC WEB

Semantics is the study of meaning. And when applied to the web, it is the meaning of one bit of content as compared to another. Semantics can be communicated to humans in a very natural visual way. But semantic code is designed to make sense to computers.

An example is by far the easiest way to help you wrap your head around this concept. Let's say you have a heading on a page; we will call it a Heading 1. You might design this heading to be a large bold type that clearly sets it up as the main heading for the page. The user will easily identify this as the main topic of the page. Examples might include About Us or What We Do. These headings communicate something about the content you are about to consume.

In a standard document-editing tool, you might set up various levels of headings from a Heading 1 to a Heading 6, all representing various degrees of hierarchy in the page. The web works the exact same way. There is a range of heading tags available to the programmer to delineate headings using specific tags. For example the <h1> tag can be used around the main heading of a page.

This is incredibly important because it relates to how the page is built. A developer could create the same large text for the main heading using a paragraph tag and apply the same CSS to create a large bold headline. It would look the same to humans, and you might think it is just fine.

This is not the case, though. The content of your site should be marked up semantically, meaning that the role of the content is clearly defined by the tags used to wrap around it. Headings should be coded using headings, paragraphs inside paragraph tags, etc.

The impact of this is simple but incredibly important. If you mark up the content of a site properly, you will by default be preparing yourself for some good search engine results. These indicators of the content's role are the primary clue that search engines will use to determine the type of content a page contains. Get this wrong and your placement in search engines will suffer.

Semantics also plays a huge role in accessibility, something we will look at next.

ACCESSIBILITY

Making the web accessible means creating sites that are usable by everyone. This includes those with vision impairments and other disabilities.

Let's consider a blind user. They will likely be using a screen reader to help them browse the web. This means that the computer will literally read the contents of a site to them. If your site is not marked up using semantic code, your users will find your site extremely frustrating. For example, if your headings don't use actual heading tags, the screen reader will have no way to read the sections to the user. This means the user will have no choice but to listen to the entire page.

Accessibility actually becomes a legal matter depending on the work you do. Some inaccessible e-commerce sites have actually been the recipients of lawsuits. And government work most often comes with the requirement that all work be accessible.

As the designer, this doesn't have a huge impact on you since you will not likely be writing the code. What it does mean though is that you should pay attention to your target audience. If you extend the idea of accessibility to apply to various demographics that are not fully disabled, you will find that you have a different perspective on how you design.

A perfect example is designing for seniors, as in people over the age of sixty-five. If this is the target audience of your site, you should carefully consider key factors such as font size, image clarity and ease of navigation. These less-code-centric issues will impact how accessible the site is to a wide variety of audiences. In this way, accessibility takes on a tremendous design role and should be carefully considered as you plan your site.

CROSS-BROWSER TESTING

A fundamental part of building websites is ensuring that they work properly across all browsers. This process has gone through various phases, and many tools have emerged to help us in our quest for full functionality.

For many years the primary goal was fairly universal: you wanted a website to render the same (or very similarly) across all browsers. But many things have changed and this is not always the case anymore. For example, some believe in the notion of graceful degradation, while others embrace responsive web design. And, of course, the influx of various devices like smartphones and tablet computers has thrown a huge wrench in the process of browser testing.

Ultimately you must form your own philosophies on how to approach browser testing. I encourage you to adapt your ideas to the individual client and their needs. Since every site is unique, it is

CROSS-BROWSER TESTING

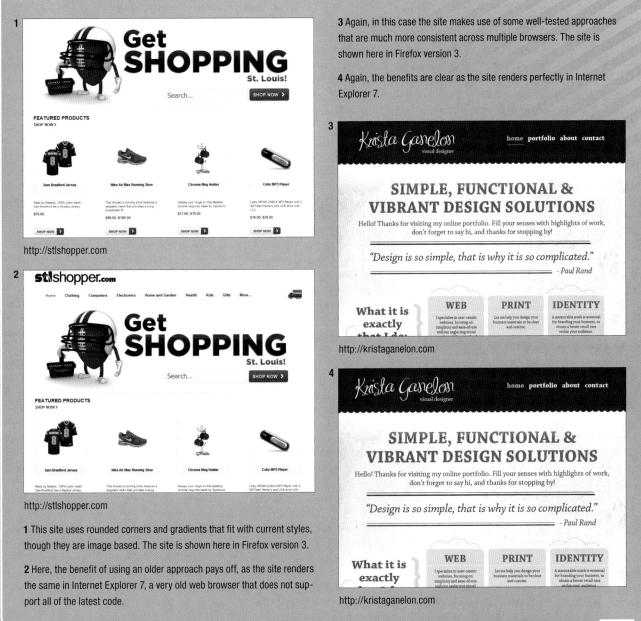

1 This site uses rounded corners and gradients that fit with current styles, though they are image based. The site is shown here in Firefox version 3.

2 Here, the benefit of using an older approach pays off, as the site renders the same in Internet Explorer 7, a very old web browser that does not support all of the latest code.

http://stlshopper.com

http://stlshopper.com

3 Again, in this case the site makes use of some well-tested approaches that are much more consistent across multiple browsers. The site is shown here in Firefox version 3.

4 Again, the benefits are clear as the site renders perfectly in Internet Explorer 7.

http://kristaganelon.com

http://kristaganelon.com

very likely that you will need to be flexible and ready to adapt your approach. Let's review two of the more popular concepts to understand how they impact the design process.

BROWSER TESTING TOOLS

When it comes time to test your site, there are two main approaches. The first is to simply get screenshots of your site in various browsers. This is a great first step and useful for quickly surveying the way your site looks. Here are some snapshot services:

Adobe Browser Lab
https://browserlab.adobe.com

This free tool from Adobe is great for full-page previews of your site. It includes side-by-side comparisons and overlay views, onion-skin style. You can also create sets of browsers to test for, which will save you time in waiting on screenshots for browsers you're not worried about.

Browsershots
http://browsershots.org

Browsershots is another free option that is rather popular and easy to use. This simple tool is a great way to quickly preview how your site renders in different browsers.

The second option is to actually use the browsers and interact with your site. Here are some tools for both approaches. One handy tool in this regard focuses on Internet Explorer:

IETester

www.my-debugbar.com/wiki/IETester/HomePage

IETester allows you to run all versions of Internet Explorer at a single time. This tool is priceless if you're trying to test older browsers in particular. When a client calls and says that the site breaks in some specific version of IE, this tool is a lifesaver.

GRACEFUL DEGRADATION

A natural part of testing a website is to ensure that it works, even if something goes wrong. Ironically, one thing that can go wrong is a user running an archaic browser. Consider if you will that you design and build a site on the latest and greatest technologies, and along comes a user still using IE 6 (an ancient browser). This old browser doesn't support many things we now do frequently.

This is where graceful degradation comes in. The goal is that when something goes wrong your site is still able to perform its necessary functions. Sometimes this means building in fall backs in case something like JavaScript is disabled. Other times it means plugging in a tool that allows an older browser to emulate a built-in feature like rounded corners.

So, as part of your browser testing, you have to go beyond simply looking at screenshots provided by snapshot services. You must actually do your best to test the site in the various browsers and platforms. Your best bet is to install as many browsers as you can for testing purposes. And be sure to check out IETester from the previous section for a great way to test multiple versions of Internet Explorer.

RESPONSIVE WEB DESIGN

Another important part of testing your site will be to make sure the site works across a number of devices. The notion of responsive web design proposes that a design should change based on the user's interface. Most often this is associated with targeting mobile, tablets and desktop computers with an appropriate layout.

This has a rather significant impact on the testing process. If you plan to build anything that targets mobile devices in any way at all, you need to be prepared to buy some devices. Identify the key targets and make sure you can actually use the device to see how it works. Nothing will beat having a real iPad and seeing how your site works.

PLATFORM-SPECIFIC CODE

As your design is cut up into code, your developer should keep your content management system in mind. The better understanding your developer has of your specific platform, the more effective he can be. Most fundamentally, this comes down to understanding the code generated by the platform. If the developer knows this well, he can make the initial conversion from design to code. Then, when you go to integrate the CSS and HTML into the platform, it will be set up and ready to go. A great example might be the way the system outputs the code for navigation menus. A developer could build the same functionality with many subtle differences in the code. If he simply uses the one that matches the platform, then the integration process will be incredibly fast and easy. If he does not, you will have to rework the code as you plug it into the system.

INTEGRATION

After your design has been translated into CSS and HTML, you will begin the process of integration. This step involves the implementation of your design as a template targeted at a specific CMS. Sometimes this part of the process will get merged with the actual slicing process; it all depends on who is doing that part of the project for you. In my experience, the results are usually cleaner if you first do the cuts and then do the integration. But that is not to say this is universally true.

An important part of the integration process is setting up a site to make maximum use of the features in the CMS. The more effectively a site is built on a CMS, the easier it will be for the site owners to maintain it. For example, a developer can simply place the main navigation into the templates and provide no way for users to add new items. Or, they can wire it up to where the list of items is managed by the CMS and content owners can easily add, remove and update items. The former is faster, but the latter is more desirable.

A great way to tell if you're not getting a quality integration into a CMS is if you have to go to the developer to have anything outside the content changed. In contrast, if you have clean access to update all parts of the site, then you are more likely getting the most out of your system.

Of course there are times when the design will create a scenario in which it can't effectively integrate with or be managed by the CMS. As you design and build sites, pay attention to these scenarios as they will help you understand where the boundaries are.

CHAPTER 7

Measuring Results

One of the greatest things about the web as a medium is how measurable everything is. To illustrate the point, consider the web in contrast to traditional print advertising.

In print, one can only estimate the number of viewers. This number can easily be up for debate—like how many people see a billboard, for example. It is also hard to measure the results of many print elements. How many people call you as a result of that billboard or magazine ad? And it is also really hard to know how people consume your print ads. What do they read first? What were they looking at before they found your ad?

In contrast, on the web we can measure all those things and more. We can track:

- The number of people that visit a site
- What content they consume
- What order they view content in
- Where they came from
- Where they leave to

- What part of the page they focus on, via mouse tracking
- How long they stay to visit
- If they take a step towards becoming a customer

The ability to measure means that we can make informed decisions unequaled in other mediums. The designers who embrace this open themselves up to a world of knowledge. The ability to help your clients make informed decisions increases your value and most likely your revenue.

GAUGING PERFORMANCE

The process of measuring begins by making something. Once you have a creation in place, you can start looking at performance. With this information in hand, you can start the process over by creating something better. This recursive process results in incremental changes that work to optimize your sites.

Many agencies work under a vastly different model. They pitch a deal, swoop in and build a website, and then disappear into the night, without any plans to measure or assess performance. In such cases, clients are only getting part of the value out of their site.

Instead, I propose that you build long-lasting relationships with your clients by helping them to measure and gauge the performance of what you build for them. The more you do this, the clearer your value to the client is. And in the end they will be long-term, happy customers.

In this section, I want to take you through the various elements that are a part of measuring the performance of your sites. We will begin with the basic idea of analytics.

USING ANALYTICS

Analytics is a topic designers either seem to love or totally disregard. In contrast, nearly every business owner loves analytics—be it website traffic data or, even better, financial analytics. Depending on the role the website plays in the company's business (informational, or a direct revenue stream), business owners would place different ranges of gravity on web analytics.

As a designer, it is critical to understand analytics and how they can be used effectively. One need not worry about every nuance of setting up Google Analytics; though actually doing it a few times is a good thing to experience. Instead, the goal is to understand what it can do other than provide some bragging points for how many visitors your work for the client brought in.

The trick is to understand the roles analytics can play, and there are two key ones to discus. The first is measuring performance. By properly assessing the past, we can gauge the effectiveness of what we have already done. I would compare this to setting a financial budget and then reviewing it at the end of the year to see how we did. You wouldn't just look at it and say we spent $1,000,000 this year. No, you would say we spent $1,000,000 of a $1.2 million budget and saved $200,000!

So, with web analytics, the goal is to look at the past in light of expectations, goals and real revenue earned. By leveraging the systems described below, you will see how your clients can begin to assess the past. More than anything, this is about putting some real numbers to things and not just "feeling" like getting 200,000 people to come to the site was enough. You will want to find yourself asking questions like: What were the goals when we started the project? What percentage growth did we achieve? What were the expectations? What was the ROI (return on investment)? Again, we're not just looking for raw numbers, but numbers in contrast to some reference point.

The second role analytics play is in looking to the future. By properly assessing the past, we can make intelligent decisions for the future. As we take the guesswork out of projects, we provide our clients with a value that will blow the doors off the competition. This is an even greater opportunity for wowing your clients because so few people even consider analytics when starting up work with a new or existing client.

Here is a really practical example. Your new client wants a slick new website. They have heard about the new developments in the industry and want to embrace the latest technology; surprisingly, they are a client ready to do something meant for the modern web. This sounds like the ideal client. But let's say you dig into their analytics and realize that a lot of their business comes from large corporations. These corporations happen to have all their users locked into Internet Explorer 6. This sort of information will hinder what is possible. But it also means you have helped the client dodge a real potential problem when their target audience doesn't get the experience they expected. This is what I call responsible design, and it wins the client over every time.

What follows are some nuances and details of how analytics can work and how the various tools can be put to work to help you guide your clients and make sound business decisions.

ANALYTICS TOOLS AND RESOURCES

Google Analytics

www.google.com/analytics

This is perhaps the biggest name in analytics (though by no means the only option). It is super simple to use, provides a ton of great data and can be extended in some very impressive ways. Best of all, it is free.

Reinvigorate

www.reinvigorate.net

There is a wide range of tools available for standard analytics; one such tool is Reinvigorate. Perhaps the single greatest reason to use this tool is its real-time stats. No need to wait until the next day to find out how your site is doing. Depending on your site, you can even track individual people and users.

SWIX Social Media Optimization

http://swixhq.com

Social media can often feel like an untrackable black hole of activity. But there are many tools to help track and monitor its effectiveness. SWIX is one such tool and comes packed with features. Track clicks, conversions and social

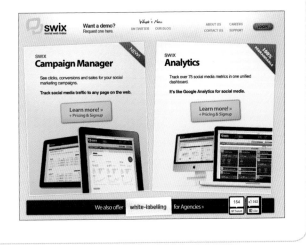

campaigns. You can also track key social metrics like followers and friend counts across numerous platforms, making it a great tool for getting a full view of your social status.

W3Schools

www.w3schools.com/browsers/browsers_stats.asp
W3Schools provides a ton of public stats for you to dig through. This allows you to understand the marketplace as a whole vs. your individual site. For example, the target audience of your site may be more inclined to use the latest browsers and devices. Or perhaps it is the opposite and your dated users fall behind. Either way, information is power.

STATISTICS

Statistics are the raw numbers most people think of when we mention the term analytics. And while stats can be very useful numbers, they are far more powerful when you put them into context. For many sites this will come naturally as you instinctively know when a basic stat is higher or lower than normal. Oftentimes though, it takes a consistent approach to reviewing these stats to make sense of them. Enter the report.

Reports are perhaps the most powerful analytics tool available. They sum up in a consistent way all of the numbers collected in the raw data. If we look at the same reports on a regular basis to check key indicators, we can really get our finger on the pulse of a website.

Let's quickly cover some of the most basic terminology when it comes to stats.

Hits

This is a tally of every single server request. This includes every file, image and asset used to load a page. One page load will incur numerous hits. Frankly speaking, hits are an irrelevant and antiquated way of looking at stats. Ignore this number.

Visits

This number represents the number of people that have visited your site. Typically, systems will distinguish between unique and total visitors. Each system has a different means of tabulating this, so you have to be cautious in comparing data from different systems. One would think that it should be easy to track this and it should be consistent, but it just isn't.

Conversions

A conversion occurs when a user takes a desired action on a site. This could be an online purchase, completion of a form or registration for a trial account, to name a few. Conversions are the primary goal of a website.

Page Views

This is the number of times a single page or all pages were viewed. This will include multiple views from the same user. This is a great indicator of the amount of data people are digging into on the site.

Collecting all of these numbers is great, and we can look at fantastic reports that give us all sorts of perspective on the usage of our websites. But the real value starts to show up as you compare these numbers. Ratios will give us better insights as we try to figure out how the numbers interrelate.

For example, we might find that our conversions are increasing—a good thing of course—but when compared to the rate of growth in unique visitors, what if we find that our growth in visitors has been much stronger? This means that, for some reason, our conversion rate is actually dropping. The goal is to understand the results of the efforts we make so we can decide what to do next. The basic idea here is that more visitors do not always mean more revenue.

One trick to stats that oftentimes gets overlooked (due to the complexity of implementing it) is the collection of extra bits of data: for example, tracking the usage of contact forms and newsletter sign-up systems. Interestingly, Google Analytics (and many other systems) lets you easily track almost any event or bit of data that you would like to.

HEAT MAPS

Heat maps are a way of viewing data in which the activity is layered over the actual site. This provides a means of visualizing data that is otherwise very difficult to understand. For example, you can look at a heat map of links clicked off the home page. This will physically show us where people are clicking.

This technique is one that has become much easier in recent years as numerous services have begun offering it up. Google Analytics has this ability built in for mapping clicks, for example. Other systems can be very quickly integrated (often with a single line of code) to start tracking such data.

This handy tool can be easy to implement and can be extremely helpful in figuring out how users interact with key parts of a site or design. Literally seeing what people are engaging with on your site can make it very easy to understand the most critical portions of your design.

A/B TESTING

A/B testing is the process of producing two alternatives to a layout or design element and comparing the results. Usually, the results being measured are the percentage of people that complete some desired action. This is most often referred to as a conversion.

Email landing pages are a perfect example. Oftentimes, email campaigns will have special landing pages on a website with the sole purpose of helping those who receive the email to take some desired action, typically to make a purchase. A popular approach is to test numerous variations on these pages until the one with the best results is found. In this way, a site owner can optimize the conversion rate. This method can be extremely powerful by impacting your client's bottom line.

SEARCH ENGINE OPTIMIZATION

Search engine optimization (or SEO) is a term that refers to the process of optimizing a site such that it maximizes free traffic sources. This is primarily focused on traffic from search engines. In the old days, you could bait the search engines in various ways, but times have changed. These days the search engines are extremely intelligent and oftentimes ruthless in penalizing those who try to game the system.

This is also a niche of the web industry that tends to get a bad rap, and for good reason, to be honest. It seems that a lot of people claim to be SEO experts after simply using a few tools to look for ways to optimize a site. Ironically, so many of the suggestions made by SEO "experts" completely contradict what the search engines have to say about their own ranking systems.

My advice to people is that there are SEO people out there who can in fact have a huge impact on your business. So go hire them. As a designer you just need to know five things that have a huge impact on SEO:

1. The most important element of SEO is high-quality original content. If you copy and paste the same content from other sites in your niche, search engines will not rank you well. In contrast, if you produce original and unique content, it will benefit you. When in doubt, or if you're just getting started, focus first on producing content. This will almost always produce the best results.

2. A good URL goes a long way. The actual structure and words used in a URL matter. Without going into too much detail, just keep in mind that the URL is your chance to place key words to closely associate with the page. And always use a hyphen (-) instead of an underscore (_) between words; the hyphen tells search engines it is two separate words.

3. Make use of page titles. Page titles are what show up in the title bar of the browser. The text here need not match the page title or the URL, though they should obviously be closely related. Again this is a chance to describe the content and place relevant words in a key part of the page.

4. In page titles, the H1, or heading 1, tag in the page is critical for good SEO. Not only that, but heading tags are good for the user, as they help her understand the content and its overall structure. Heading tags in HTML documents are much like those in a Microsoft Word document. The coder has access to H1 through H6 tags, and making use of these is a fundamental part of building a good website.

5. The meta description tag is the only one that matters. Meta tags are hidden tags that show up in the beginning of a web page. In the past, meta tags were *the* thing to do for good SEO, but nowadays you only need to be concerned with the description tag. Google, for example, has publicly stated for some time that it ignores the meta keyword tag.

DATA-DRIVEN DESIGN

One of the natural results of working with data is that it can actually drive the design process. While it might not seem like a very creative process, it does make good business sense. It is important to keep in mind the purpose of the site you're working on. Most likely it is intended to contribute to a revenue stream.

The good news is that it doesn't have to be purely scientific. Yes, you might use the data to figure out which of two designs works better.

But someone had to create those two alternatives. Just look at data-driven design work as a type of work with some constraints. It certainly doesn't mean it has to be ugly or ignore the normal design process.

DESIGN, MEASURE, REPEAT

When doing data-driven design work, you will often follow the formula of design, measure and repeat. This process is not about doing it once; rather, it is about repeating the cycle over and over. The net result is that you squeeze all of the optimization you can out of the design. An important thing to keep in mind when you do this sort of work is to take many small steps instead of large radical ones. So don't radically change everything on a page and then test it for results. Doing so will result in data that is hard to interpret in contrast to the original design. You want to slowly change things and see how it goes. Some changes you will want to scrap and revert to the prior version. Others will produce positive results that you will keep.

Repeating this cycle many times is a common practice for sales-driven sites. You will find this especially true on e-commerce sites. It is also useful for any site that drives users to a clear and measurable conversion point.

A great example of this might be a button on a home page that drives users to sign up for a free trial. You can slightly alter countless attributes—for example, placement, color, size and wording—over time and see how they impact the end results. Tweak one of these and measure the results. Then repeat.

The beauty of this is that it helps you maximize the traffic you're already getting. An argument that is frequently made is that it is often easier to increase the conversion rate of existing visitors instead of acquiring new ones. Even better, do both!

CRITICAL PATHS

An important concept to keep in mind when it comes to analytics and assessing the performance of a site is that of critical paths. A critical path includes the key steps a visitor must take in order to complete a conversion. A perfect example of this is in the e-commerce world. Let's view the steps in such a process.

The visitor lands on the site and must do the following:

1. View a product
2. Add a product to the cart
3. Visit the shopping cart page
4. Begin the checkout process
5. Land on the checkout confirmation page

A user that completes this entire process has made it through a critical path. Some sites will have much shorter critical paths, but the important thing to do is identify the path. With the path in mind, you will be able to measure the activity and make appropriate decisions.

MEASURING USAGE AND ACTIVITY

Almost every type of site has a critical path; you simply have to understand what it is. As a result, you will want to measure and track its performance. This is a key step in the design, measure and repeat cycle.

Let's say for example you begin tracking the critical path mentioned earlier. Perhaps you find that many people make it into the checkout process, but very few complete it. This can help you identify a weak point in your site that you need to address. By understanding the activity, you can make effective decisions on where to focus your energy.

CONVERSION TRACKING

Most analytics tools include the ability to track conversions. But don't limit yourself to only considering literal purchases with a conversion. There are many things that can and should be considered a conversion.

Consider a standard brochure site for a handyman. Perhaps this site does not have anything to sell directly on the site, but there are many things that could be considered conversion points. Perhaps the site has a contact or quote request form. These simple elements are a critical step in the visitor becoming a paying customer and should be tracked as key conversion points.

Another thing to keep in mind is that a site might have many ways of accomplishing a conversion. Perhaps you have an email newsletter; a user registering for it has taken a key step in the path to becoming a converted user.

Talk to your clients and understand what will make their site a success. By doing so you will identify your critical paths and what will be considered a conversion point. As a result, you will be far better informed in how to design for them and how to help them succeed. And, of course, this is how you truly help clients and build lasting relationships.

INFORMED DECISIONS
AND STRATEGIC UPDATES

The ultimate goal when it comes to analytics is to make informed decisions. Instead of randomly deciding what to do, you look at the data and make decisions that are most likely to help your client.

Informed decisions lead to better results. Some examples of potential things to add or revise on a site:

"What content do most people use on our site?"
Analytics tells us the most popular pages.

"Should I create a special mobile version of my site?"
Check analytics to see what devices people are using.

"What pages lose the most viewers?"
Look into your analytics to see what pages most frequently end a user's visit to your site.

"What sections should I expand?"
Again, dig into the data and find out what sections people view most; perhaps this is where you should invest more energy.

There are countless questions to ask, but the point is simple: if we leverage the data we collect, we can make for more strategic and valuable updates. In e-commerce, it can be a lot easier to understand where to invest your time and energy, but the same basic ideas apply across all types of sites.

PROCESS IS GOOD FOR EVERYONE

Working this way is good for everyone. At first it might not feel like the most "creative" way to work, but I would argue otherwise. Working online is about business, not creativity (most of the time anyway), so making smart business decisions should be the goal.

GOOD FOR BUSINESS

This approach is actually really good for the designers. Without any data, you can feel lost as to where to turn or what to propose that a client improve about their site. Analyzing the data can be a great way to figure out where to head next, and it can provide a financial incentive to the client.

Best of all, if you focus your energy on learning how to help clients make good choices, you will make yourself more valuable. If every time you engage your clients you're helping them make more money, they will love you. This will make it a very easy for them to return to you for more help in the future.

If instead you simply show up and do some fancy work with no sense of goals, past performance or business strategy, your work will be of less value. Focus on helping your clients make good business decisions and you will no doubt succeed.

RINSE AND REPEAT

The great thing about this approach is that the entire process repeats. So, rather than doing one of the projects with no plan for more, you're approaching your work in a way that builds repeat business from the get go.

   This analytical approach is so often overlooked, and yet it can lead to valuable long-term relationships. If you can build measurements into the work you do, I am certain you will find that it is not only empowering but also highly profitable.

CHAPTER 8

Maintenance: A Long-Term Strategy

An important aspect of any website is day-to-day maintenance. Some sites will sit for years without any changes or updates. But this is not the case for most business sites. Maintenance becomes a major point of concern and is a critical element to consider when designing and building a site.

Not only do we need to understand how to design in such a way that allows our creation to come to life in code, but we must also consider how it can grow, change and live over time. It is quite possible to design and build a site that is so difficult to maintain that it must simply be replaced far faster than necessary.

An ideal design will not only look great today but will also accommodate for changes over time. What follows are some of the most critical topics to consider when planning for ongoing maintenance.

WEB-SAFE TYPE

A very basic limitation of designing for the web is the fonts available to be used. There are, of course, many ways around this limitation.

But we must understand the basic options available prior to exploring more complex solutions. (See page 198 for samples.)

Font limitations are due to the fact that font information is not embedded in a web page, as it might be in a PDF containing any font required. This means you are relying on an individual's computer to have the selected font installed. If the specified font is not available, it won't be able to render, and it will use a system default font instead. This means that fonts considered web safe are those found on most computers (and devices) by default. Obviously this seriously limits the range of options pretty quickly.

Here is a list of fonts commonly considered web-safe:

- Arial
- Georgia
- Times New Roman
- Verdana
- Courier
- Tahoma
- Arial Black
- Trebuchet
- Lucida
- Palatino
- Impact

Again, there are many ways around the limitation of font selection, which we explore next. The real point with the list of web-safe fonts

www.dangrossman.info

1 All the type on this site, except the title, is entirely web safe. No plug-ins or extensions are required. The site's speed, clean design and clarity make up for any lack of visual pizzazz.

2 This design consists almost entirely of web-safe type and proves that, though limiting, the short list of fonts available can still be used in beautiful ways.

www.pixelflips.com

is that they are the easiest to implement. We need not use any coding trickery; we simply specify the font and it works.

EXTENDED FONTS WITH @FONT-FACE

There are a number of ways to embed custom fonts in a website. We will begin with the @font-face tag. Let's start from the beginning. @font-face is a set of CSS tags we use to declare a custom font inside our style sheets. Once defined and properly linked to, we can simply apply the new font to text as needed in our styles. (See page 200 for samples.)

This approach to embedding custom fonts has quickly become one of the most popular. It is relatively simple to implement, it has great browser support (though not universal) and it runs very quickly with only minimal performance implications. If I were to suggest a single approach, this would be it.

These tags are a bit complicated to generate by hand, but as usual, there are some extremely helpful tools that totally automate the process. Check out the sidebar for more information on these utilities.

In regards to maintenance, this approach is simply fabulous. Since the font is applied through standard CSS calls, there are no difficult hoops to jump through. One can simply update text as needed and the font is applied.

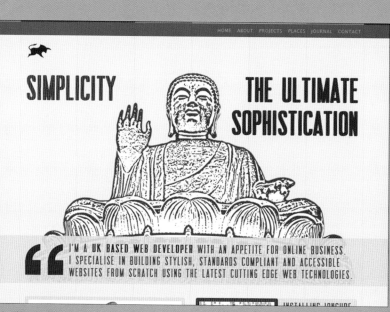

http://davebrookes.com

1 The custom typography on this page is powered by standard CSS @font-face techniques.

2 Many of the most fantastic uses of custom fonts are subtle solutions such this one.

3 The text on this site feels completely normal, and the extended font embedded in the site blends perfectly with the design.

www.futuretap.com

www.webcoursesbangkok.com

WEB FONT SERVICES

Font Squirrel
www.fontsquirrel.com

This should be your first stop for getting started with @font-face–based text styles. This tool basically does all the hard work for you. It provides all of the needed files and CSS styles required to get going. Seriously, this service just makes custom fonts as simple as they can possibly be.

Typekit
http://typekit.com

Typekit is a commercial alternative to the free options available. This service offers licensing that allows you to leverage a wide range of fonts beyond the free options. Depending on your project, paying for custom fonts may very well be a viable option. One huge upside to services like Typekit is that they make the whole process even easier by hosting the font files on their servers; simply plug in a bit of code and you're off and running.

Google Web Fonts API
http://code.google.com/apis/webfonts

Google also offers a convenient and free font delivery service that easily allows developers to use fonts on sites. This service's biggest limitation used to be the range of fonts it offered, but with an ever-growing list of options, it is rapidly becoming a great tool to keep in mind.

IMAGE REPLACEMENT

One of the oldest techniques for displaying text in custom type faces on the web is to replace standard text with an image of the text. With the recent wave of interest in actual live text styled with CSS-based @font-face techniques, this age-old method has fallen out of focus. Yes, the days of generating an image of every page title are over, but that doesn't mean this approach is no longer viable.

There are many situations in which you might want to have total control over a bit of text by placing it in an image. For example, say you have a very specialized layout on your home page with some large text. Depending on the design, this might be the best approach.

Given that this is a section on maintenance, I want to provide some insights from such a perspective. By placing text in an image, you inevitably create a maintenance problem. If ever the text is to be updated, someone will have to modify the file and export a new JPEG or PNG. This means you have to have access to the font files and the original layered Photoshop document. Not a huge deal, but these sorts of files have a way of disappearing.

This approach is a 100 percent valid option to use. Just keep in mind that maintenance and development will be a bit more painful. So don't design a site that requires the main heading of every page be exported as a static image. This approach is ideal for limited situations where a specific style is required.

IMAGE REPLACEMENT

1 The custom type in this heading is more manageable as an image. It is also the type of content that is seldom updated, so it works out great.

2 Large text like this is a prime candidate for image replacement, as it allows the designer total control over the spacing of the letters, words and lines.

3 While the effects on this text could be replicated in CSS3, it is oftentimes easier to use an image.

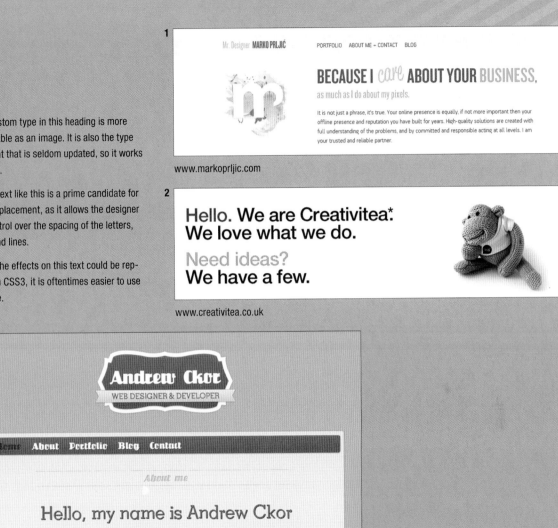

www.markoprljic.com

www.creativitea.co.uk

www.andrewckor.com

FONT REPLACEMENT

The final technique we will cover here for implementing a custom font is what I would consider the most difficult to explain. There are several approaches, but in one way or another it involves replacing text in a page with alternate elements. The two most popular approaches make use of Flash (via sIFR) and JavaScript (via cufon).

Basically the page loads and the tool dynamically replaces the text with the technology it is based on. So, for example, with sIFR, the page loads as normal. Then a special JavaScript routine runs, replacing specific text with a Flash movie. This movie contains the correct font and dynamically adjusts to the actual text in the page.

This is very similar to replacing text with an image, but with some clear differences. First of all, you have far less control. If you are rendering some large fancy text with an image you can carefully control every aspect of word, letter and line spacing. These elements are perfectly preserved in the image you export. In contrast, text rendered using font replacement is rendered using the same settings no matter what.

The second big difference is that image-based text is hard to update, whereas text rendered with font replacement is 100 percent updateable. Since the text is rendered in the user's browser, you can simply update the actual text in the page and the results flow into the correct font. Ease of maintenance is why this approach has been incredibly popular.

Prior to recent developments with CSS-based @font-face approaches, font replacement was king. The approach is not altogether a thing of the past, but it does appear that @font-face–based approaches are

FONT REPLACEMENT

1 The use of font replacement here allows the text to be easily updated while fitting the style of the site.

www.getsyncd.com

quickly fading. Frankly speaking, I was on the fence in regards to even including this technique, but I decided it was worth including to ensure you were aware of the history. It might also help should you have to work on a site that still uses it, which is, of course, a lot of sites.

DESIGNING WITHIN LIMITATIONS

One of the most basic stumbling blocks for designers new to the web is figuring out how to embrace the limitations of the medium. By working within the limitations of the web, designers have a chance to really impact the ongoing costs of maintaining a website, not to mention the initial production costs. In many ways this is really the core purpose of this book, to educate designers on how to understand the web and work *with* it.

We cannot approach the web with creative outlet as the primary goal. As I mentioned earlier, I think a fantastic comparison is to the automotive industry. Car designers can exercise a lot of creativity, but they have some very basic limitations. Cars have certain norms that must be followed, such as they have four wheels, drivers must sit on a standard side and doors belong on the side of the vehicle.

Even more importantly, consider the usability limitations. Door handles must be reachable, dashboard gauges must be readable and seats must accommodate for a wide range of heights and widths of passengers.

An automotive designer has constraints, as do web designers. The difference is that on the web it sometimes feels like we can build anything we can imagine. Which in many cases is true, but it is not always practical.

If we learn to embrace the limitations of the web, we will create sites that are easier to build, save our clients time and money and most importantly accomplish their mission effectively.

I am not against Flash at all; I believe it is a fantastic tool that has many great uses. But, when designers approach the web with creativity as the main goal, you most often end up with a design that can only be implemented with Flash. Allowing creative demands to completely detach from the technical implications is not desirable, nor is it an effective way to build websites.

Instead, I propose we plan the project, sort out what the best possible structure is, and then see what technologies might fit the bill. Design conceived within the limitations of the project, the technologies and the needs of the client will lead to better results in the long run, and such an understanding leads to greater control over the costs of maintaining and owning a website.

FLASH AND JQUERY

When it comes to site maintenance, it is important to consider what technologies will be put to work. Two of the most popular front-end tools for accomplishing advanced functionality are Flash and jQuery. (See page 209 for samples.)

In many ways these two can be interchangeable. For example, there are lots of awesome Flash-based photo gallery tools, and likewise, there are countless jQuery-based options. Certainly there are situations where one does things the other struggles to replicate, but in many ways they are nothing more than tools to accomplish various tasks.

In keeping with this chapter's theme of site maintenance, I want to focus a bit of energy on the topic. Both of these tools allow for slick functionality but come at the potential cost of maintenance.

Let's start with Flash. For starters, Flash movies are compiled and can only be updated if you have the original source file. This alone can make maintenance more difficult. But there are methods for creating dynamic Flash movies that load content users can more easily maintain.

On the jQuery side, you find a similar problem. jQuery plug-ins run off standard HTML. The trick is that this code typically has very specific needs. It often must be structured a specific way, with specific classes and IDs. This isn't so hard for those familiar with HTML, but it can be very difficult for anyone else.

These tools are used heavily, so I just want to ensure you understand the implications. They oftentimes present a long-term maintenance issue you must account for. Plan for this ahead of time by accommodating a means to update them with foolproof tools or budget with your clients for the time to perform the work. This leads to the idea of a CMS perfectly, so let's dive in there.

MAINTAINING CMS-BASED SITES

These tools are intended to allow content contributors to easily update and publish content. From a site maintenance standpoint, this is the only way to go.

Building a website on a CMS will increase the costs of building the site, but in the long run it will reduce the cost of maintenance and site ownership. This makes it an important part of the building of a modern site and a critical component to fully explore.

FLASH AND JQUERY

1 Dynamic sites like this one would have previously been built using Flash but now are built often on HTML and JavaScript.

2 This site's interactive approach echoes techniques previously accomplished with Flash.

www.drkrush.com

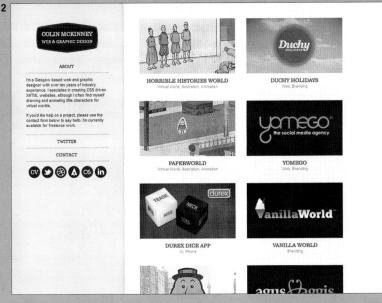

www.colinmckinney.co.uk

USING TEMPLATES

An important part of building sites on a CMS is the use of templates. The idea is that not every single page should be custom built from the ground up. Instead, you will build page templates that can be reused over and over. This saves a lot of time and allows content to be more easily published.

As you design pages consider how they can be turned into reusable templates. To do this, consider how your design will work as things change. What if there is a really long heading or title? What if the content shrinks or grows? What if I need to add more navigation options?

REPEATABLE CONTENT AND LAYOUTS

As you begin designing with reusable templates in mind, you will inevitably come across some content that repeats, such as a list of products, a list of store locations or a list of company employees. These lists of content create an opportunity for easy maintenance. (See page 212 for samples.)

When designing a list of repeated items, you should consider how consistent you are in the list. The more variance you create among the items, the more costly it will be to build and it will be harder to maintain. If every item has customized elements or varying layouts, it will just be a lot more difficult to work with.

This is not meant to squash creativity. As with all things, you can certainly design a very custom layout for every item of a list. The idea is to simply understand that it will drive costs up and be more difficult to maintain.

TEMPLATES

http://scentsybuddy.com

1 While the design of this site is gorgeous, it doesn't lend itself to the most repeatable of formats that would accommodate a wide range of content.

2 This design is visually intense, but the text and images are contained in ways that allow them to easily expand and change. This makes it very flexible for future content.

3 This gorgeous design is perfectly set up to allow for a wide range of content. This makes it a great template and gives the site a longer shelf life.

www.reading-riding-retrofit.org

http://daytonfarmersmarket.com

REPEATABLE CONTENT AND LAYOUTS

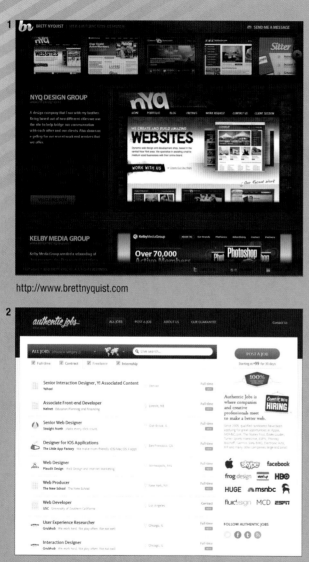

http://www.brettnyquist.com

http://authenticjobs.com

1 The large portfolio items in this list repeat in layout and are perfect to set up as repeating dynamic content.

2 Sites like this have to be dynamic, so an extremely consistent format is used to ease the coding and maintenance of the site.

3 The grid of items here are completely consistent without any unique attributes to any individual element. This makes them easy to code against.

http://williamsnash.com

WORKING WITH DATABASES

The notion of repeatable content leads us to an important maintenance topic. Quite often, repeating content will be stored in a database. Then, special code will be used to retrieve the data and dynamically generate the HTML for the user to view. This makes generating the code faster, more accurate and easier to update.

The thing to realize is that if you store data in a database, you will need a way to allow users to update, delete and add new items. This is not that hard to accomplish, but it does add to the costs of building the site.

This is another reason it becomes important to minimize custom variations in a list of items. Each minor change or custom element will have to be accommodated for in a database, as well as in the code to output the page.

This sort of functionality is basically a mini custom CMS and is a great approach to building websites. It is just important to understand that it takes time to implement.

REPLICATION: CAN WE REUSE ANY ASSETS?

Another aspect of building templates that becomes very economical is building reusable elements. Let's say for example you are designing a site that will have a row of three callout elements. Perhaps these same elements will need to be in a vertical sidebar on subpages of the site. A simple way to save money will be to design the sidebar of the subpages to match the width of the home page elements. This way the element can be coded once and simply reused. As simple as this sounds, it is actually very easy to overlook.

The more you begin to think in this way, the more you will start to visualize the elements of your designs as modules that can be used over and over. This is much better than seeing every page layout of a site as an independent design.

This approach is easy to think about at times, like headers and footers, but very easy to overlook for individual elements of a site. From a maintenance and cost-of-ownership standpoint, the more you design with reusable elements in mind, the more you will be able to build profit into your projects.

This whole idea can also extend beyond a single site to all the projects you work on. If you build on a standard grid size across projects, you will eventually develop many elements and overall layouts that you can call on. This saves you time, and again, lets you or your agency make higher margins.

Frankly, this is one of the simplest ways to work efficiently. It is also one of the most neglected approaches.

SCALABILITY AND CONTENT

When it comes to planning for site maintenance, scalability is an incredibly important factor. As you plan your site, you can only assume that the site will change over time; and most often this means it will grow to be larger.

There are many ways to consider scalability, depending on your specific site, so I will focus my energy on the two most common.

First, ensure that your navigation can grow over time. Horizontal, tab-style navigation is very popular, but you can quickly run out of room. Most often the main tabs of a site are fixed, and

SCALABILITY AND CONTENT

1 This home page could be made to expand vertically, but the three equal-height columns lock the page into a more rigid format.

2 In contrast to the home page, this content page can easily grow to accommodate any length of content.

http://karijobe.com

http://karijobe.com

1

http://collisionlabs.com

1 This home page is fairly flexible, though somewhat locked into the current format without intervention from a designer and developer.

2 In contrast to the home page, this content page is set up to allow for almost any content the site might need to include.

2

http://collisionlabs.com

it is the sub-sections that are allowed to more easily grow. These subsections are most typically displayed in a vertical list of links. In this way, they can easily accommodate for many pages. Certainly not every site takes this approach, but it is a common solution that allows for growth.

The second thing to plan for is content that changes and grows over time. Make sure that you plan how your design will stretch and grow should the content become longer than expected. Also consider the reverse: Does your design hold up if a page with very little text is produced?

PLANNING FOR MORE

Planning for more on every front will help you build more efficient systems and will pump more value into the work you do. Plan for more content and allow your designs to expand and scale. Plan to allow users to add and update content by using a CMS. Plan for future designs by preparing a common grid system that helps you build reusable modules.

You should plan for more in many ways, because inevitably there will be more! It might sound silly, but there are many designers that approach every project on its own and oftentimes fail to plan for the ever-changing content of a site.

CONCLUSION

One of the most difficult things about this book for me is that I want you to know and learn everything all at once. But, of course, that is impossible. I encourage you to review sections of this book as you encounter them in your everyday work. I really believe that you will get more and more out of each part of this process as you begin to understand all the other parts.

The entire process is most certainly a complex one. It involves numerous technologies, many areas of expertise and countless contradicting options. In the end, the better you understand the medium, the better you can make it work for you. And I truly believe that through better understanding you will enhance the value you bring to clients and the agencies you work for.

APPENDIX A

WordPress 101

by Jesse Friedman

Simply put, WordPress is the most important CMS available. Yes, there are tons of awesome alternatives. Many of these, in various situations, will be better choices. However, WordPress is so universal and extremely flexible that it can solve the vast majority of situations we face. This platform powers a staggering number of websites. And designers who embrace this platform set themselves up to be valuable assets in countless situations. WordPress is the Internet equivalent to Microsoft Word; consider how universal MS Word has become. You will find that oftentimes familiarity with WordPress is actually assumed.

The following section is written by Jesse Friedman. He is a teacher, designer and developer with a primary focus on working with Word-Press. As such, he is the perfect person to provide an in-depth intro-duction to WordPress and to explain many of the fundamental parts of WordPress.

DIGGING INTO WORDPRESS

Arriving at WordPress.com, you will find today's public stats proudly displaying that hundreds of thousands of bloggers have written somewhere close to a *billion* words using WordPress. In fact, WordPress powers millions of websites through their hosted system and downloadable software. It has been reported that WordPress powers 54 percent of sites using a known CMS, which is roughly 14 percent of all websites (http://w3techs.com/technologies/details/cm-wordpress/all/all). This platform is insanely popular and is an important tool to learn if you want to play on the modern web.

WordPress is a free, open-source piece of software and has many resources available to help. Where WordPress stands out is in its amazing community of users, designers and developers. This community has done just about anything and everything imaginable to the platform. As a result, there is a wealth of knowledge, plug-ins, templates and various tools that make WordPress such a flexible platform. WordPress is FREE, and you're encouraged to play, modify and mutate WordPress however you want. The end result is a huge marketplace for work of many types all around this single platform.

Whether you're a blogger on WordPress.com or a small business with WordPress installed on your own server, a theme designer or a plug-in developer, there is a huge and eager WordPress community available to help you answer questions, plan your projects and accomplish your goals.

Because of the WordPress community, and the fact that many designers and developers contribute their designs and code to the WordPress Directory, we have an extremely large amount of plug-ins and themes available to us. WordPress.org has two significant and very large directories, one for plug-ins currently hosting more than 15,000 plug-ins, and one for themes, with more than 1,400 available. These directories offer free and powerful resources. There are also countless premium themes and plug-ins built specifically for Word-Press scoured across the Internet.

WordPress started as a blogging platform, but it has grown well beyond that. Thanks to various extensions and plug-ins, the platform has been turned into everything from a social media tool to a full-blown e-commerce portal. It is this extreme flexibility that makes WordPress such a critical tool in the modern web professional's tool belt.

WordPress.com hosts your blog for free, and at this moment, your WordPress.com blog is one of 25 million. In other words, there are approximately 50 million WordPress websites out there and about half of them are hosted on WordPress.com. The advantage of Word-Press.com is that you don't have to pay for hosting or worry about security or downtime or any of the other headaches that arise from managing a website. The downfall is that your customization is greatly reduced because you're only able to choose from a limited number of themes and plug-ins. At this time, you cannot upload your own theme or other code to the WordPress.com network. However, you can utilize your own custom domain instead of relying on the default companyname.wordpress.com URL.

WordPress.org allows you to download your own copy of Word-Press to install on your own servers. Utilizing the WordPress software on your server opens the customization doors and allows you to build anything. Of course, anytime you host a system like this yourself, you have to maintain it, so you should carefully consider if this is the right tool for you.

Installing WordPress on your server takes about five minutes (no joke, it's actually famous for its "5 minute install," which you can read about here: http://codex.wordpress.org/Installing_WordPress). In fact, many web-hosting services actually offer one-click installs, where you can literally have an installed copy of WordPress at the click of the mouse. Once it's installed on your server, you can extend your WordPress CMS with plug-ins and themes, adding functionality and changing the design of your site. Installing plug-ins and themes are as simple as dropping them in their relative folders in your server directory, then going into your WordPress Admin area and "activating" them. Or, you can simply use the interface inside your WordPress admin area to install them on the fly. It is an extremely simple process to get started with. It's so easy, in fact, that there is no real excuse not to try it out and get familiar with it.

Now that you know how big WordPress is, let's talk about why you should design for it and how to get started.

GETTING TO KNOW WORDPRESS

As a designer, you should become aware of the tools WordPress has to offer so you know what functionality you can leverage and what areas require more work for the developer. If you read my bio, you'll see that I carry a few different torches. I teach web design and development at a university in Rhode Island, but I also work for an agency and do freelance on the side. As a freelancer, I work solo on all projects and design and develop everything. This makes my life easy because as I'm designing any site, I'm also writing code in my head. I know exactly how I will code a page before I even finish the design.

However, I also work at an agency, and at this agency I only develop. My design team also only does design. In other words, while we work hand in hand, there has been a lot of learning on both sides of the team to understand each other and why we need things done a certain way.

Since my designers have never coded a site, let alone a WordPress theme, the challenge becomes knowing how to lay out a dynamic site while harnessing all the available functionalities of WordPress. The biggest hurdle has been helping the designers realize that we should not design for content, but rather design layouts that content can easily fit into. This is a subtle shift that is hard to pick up on, and it can be rather frustrating. Think of it this way: You may be designing the page today, for the content you have today. But the content will change, and perhaps look totally different someday. So, if you design a site that provides for styles and layouts that can change over time, then the design will work over a much greater period of time. This longer life span makes the design work you do far more valuable. This is especially true when it comes to themes (themes being site templates that are intended to be reused for other websites). In these, we have to have a flexible layout that can compensate for all sorts of content.

KEEP A DYNAMIC MIND-SET

Whether you're designing a site for a specific company or product that happens to be powered by WordPress or you're designing a theme that is going to be available to the world to be used and abused, you have to think dynamically. This means you have to assume things will change. Content will grow and shrink. Content owners will add images, create new pages and extend navigation on the site. Accommodating for the changes your original design will undergo involves thinking dynamically. The term *dynamic* is used because a good WordPress theme is made to be dynamic. So things like the navigation are controlled by the platform based on content entered by the users. One thing I've learned over the years is that you can't possibly predict what a site will become, and if you empower clients to control their own content through a CMS like WordPress, they are going to break things. They are going to add twenty navigation items to the header, or a YouTube video that is wider than the column you designed for it. It's inevitable and frankly should be expected. Some things you need not plan for or fix, while at the same time, you should always build a degree of flexibility into your designs.

PAGE TEMPLATES ARE YOUR FRIENDS

WordPress makes it very easy to design for multiple page types, and that is one of the features that makes this platform so incredible. Typically in any web design you have the home page layout and then various internal page layouts. WordPress makes it very easy to create an unlimited number of templates to allow users to find the best layout for their content, rather than you trying to design for their content.

This may feel unnatural and rather tough to swallow. As a designer, you care about every pixel and you want the layout of line of text to be absolutely perfect. When we are working with dynamic sites, you have to remember that the content is going to change, and most companies will not have the budget or the time for you to lay out every page of content before they put it live.

Instead, you can create different layouts for the user to choose from. For them it's a simple as choosing the correct template from a drop-down in the WordPress backend. For a developer, it's as simple as declaring the template in the PHP file they code out. For you, it's the closest you're going to get to maintaining design control over the site.

GALLERIES AND MEDIA/THUMBNAILS

One of my favorite features in WordPress is that you can define how and when to use media throughout the site. Let's say you have a client using your theme and they want to write a post about their cat Chaco. They have a great photo of Chaco playing with his favorite toy.

At this point, your client doesn't care what it took for you to design this site, or that theme is powered by thousands of lines of code. The world begins and ends right now with getting that picture of Chaco on the Internet. On top of that, your theme is using posted images three different ways: (1) on the home page, where the image is 250px × 250px; (2) on archive and search result pages, you're showing an excerpt of the post and a 100px × 100px thumbnail; (3) on the actual post, where we're presented with a 600px × 350px image featured above all the content.

We know that giving your user instructions on how to resize this image and post it three different ways is going to be pointless. Instead, we can utilize the built-in "featured image" functionality in WordPress. The developer can simply "activate" the featured images and define the names and sizes of all the thumbnails we're going to be using. Now, once the client uploads that photo of Chaco, the photo will automatically be resized into all three of our dimensions and made available to the theme for showing our users. We've just eliminated a ton of work for everyone from the designer to the end user.

PAGINATION (FORWARD AND BACK, OR ARROWS)

To demonstrate the complete flexibility of this system, let's get creative with pagination. All too often, we see a series of numbers with a "back" and "next" button surrounding them. Since WordPress is so flexible, it's really quite simple to modify the built-in pagination tools and create some fun alternatives. Instead of that basic text, think about using arrows, hands pointing or other graphics. We can also get creative with the wording and start saying things like "Forward in Time" vs. "Back in Time."

While pagination as a whole is a quick topic, it speaks to the volume of customization that is available throughout WordPress. These types of changes allow for you to take complete control of your site.

DYNAMIC AND SCALABLE MENUS

Menus are a relatively new feature to WordPress and already I don't know how we lived without them. Site administrators can now create entire menus with hierarchies including pages, categories and external links. This functionality makes life very easy for site owners, but it can be a bit challenging for designers. Not only do you have to compensate for menus being dynamic but also scalable. In other words, your design, which was made to hold four navigation items in the header, may quickly be filled with a dozen or more links with children and even grandchildren.

Menus can be coded anywhere in your theme, and you can even define a menu before the admin has had a chance to create it. Menus are most commonly used in the header, footer and sidebars (widget areas). Drop-downs should be designed to hold at least one tier of children, if not two. Your developer can put a cap on the children in a navigation menu so you don't have to compensate for great-grandchildren in your header.

A common practice at my agency is to create a navigation menu in the header that only has one or two tiers and then later we allow for full-tiered menus in the sidebar. We do this because no amount of training will keep a client from adding great-great-great-grandchild menu items.

There are countless other features in WordPress, but the best way to get to know them is to play around for yourself. I highly encourage you to set up your own WordPress site and play with the admin panel to see what is possible.

MAKING MONEY DESIGNING FOR WORDPRESS

Since WordPress powers nearly half of all websites with a content management system, it makes sense to learn how to design for it. At the same time, there are ways you can think a bit more aggressively about making money with the most popular CMS available. Below are some of the more popular ideas for increasing revenue, but many of them require a developer to turn your designs into a living, breathing site. I suggest you find yourself a great WordPress developer or start writing some code. As an experienced coder, it's hard for me to tell you how easy it is to get started with WordPress development. And of all the CMSes I have trained my students on, WordPress has been the most fun and easy for them to learn.

DESIGN THEMES FOR NOTORIETY

Creating a theme and posting it to the free WordPress theme directory can get you a lot of attention, especially if you do a great job. It also feels good to contribute to a community like WordPress.

DESIGN THEMES FOR RESALE

There are too many WordPress "Foundries" to count at the moment. The most popular are Elegant Themes (www.elegantthemes.com), Woo Themes (www.woothemes.com) and Theme Forest (www.themeforest.net). These sites offer premium themes for sale and can be a great way to test the market for your designs.

Position yourself as a WordPress designer. Specializing in specific niches may limit your project availability but it also puts you at a higher level than your competition. If I know I want a WordPress site, I'm more likely to choose a WordPress designer than a generic web designer. Not to mention that the more familiar you are with this platform, the more effective your designs will be.

IN CONCLUSION

I encourage you to play and have fun with WordPress. Enjoy the built-in tools and the functionality available to you. Check out the source code from themes and plug-ins and see what others are doing. It also makes sense to find some premium themes that include PSD files when you purchase the theme. Elegant Themes does this and it really helps to tear apart someone's work to see how they did it.

ABOUT JESSE FRIEDMAN

Jesse Friedman built his first website in 1999 and has been doing it ever since. After receiving a degree in web management and Internet commerce, he founded SWORD Studios. Jesse dedicated his efforts at SWORD Studios to educating and helping the web industry and small local businesses succeed online.

Today Jesse is a professor at Johnson & Wales University, shaping young designer and developer minds. Jesse is also the lead developer at ngeni.us, a division of Neal Advertising, where they build online web environments powered by WordPress.

Jesse has a passion for WordPress, responsive web design and web standards. Jesse contributes to the WordPress community online as a developer and offline as an organizer of WordPress meetups and a speaker at conferences. He continues to challenge himself and others to be the best web designers/developers they can be. You can find Jesse online at http://jesserfriedman.com or on Twitter @professor.

The Myth of DPI

by Ben Gremillion

Most designers are familiar with the term DPI, or dots per inch. It is a topic that can be remarkably confusing, despite how simple the idea is in concept. This is perhaps especially true when it comes to those transitioning from print.

On the web, DPI is a radically different beast. As I researched this topic for the book, I ran across a wonderful article on Web Designer Depot by Ben Gremillion. And though I summed it up as you have perhaps read in the section "Design at 72dpi" in chapter 5 on page 110, I felt his article simply did a far better job at providing a truly complete explanation. So, fortunately Ben agreed to have his article included here. I think you will find it to be an in-depth and complete explanation of DPI and how it impacts web design.

The original article can be found here:

www.webdesignerdepot.com/2010/02/the-myth-of-dpi

THE MYTH OF DPI

The size of an image in a website layout is important. From proper alignment to getting *just* the right amount of white space, sizing photos and graphics properly beforehand is essential to creating a balanced look.

Images on the web are measured in pixels. Yet many people go through the trouble of setting their images to 72 dots per inch (dpi). The process of sizing images for the web is often misunderstood.

The misconception about resolution in digital images bound for the web is that they must meet a certain number of dots per inch.

In print, pixels per inch and dots per inch impact the size of an image on a page. *DPI doesn't apply to layout on the web in the same way.*

When someone converts an image to 72dpi, they're adding an extra step with no benefit. Web pages are measured in pixels, not real-world units such as inches.

When someone asks you for a web image that's, say, two inches wide, they're estimating how it would appear on their own monitor. Without changing the image's pixel dimensions, that image would appear larger or smaller on different monitors—and would even look different on the same monitor at a different resolution setting.

PIXEL SIZE DEPENDS ON CONTEXT

A pixel (which is short for "picture element") is the smallest unit of measurement on a grid displaying a digital image. DPI measures how big those pixels, or dots, are when they're printed. When applied to the web, an image will display at the same size regardless of DPI, if the actual pixel dimensions are the same.

If you want to change an image's size, you must resample it.

RESIZING CHANGES PIXEL SIZES; RESAMPLING CHANGES PIXEL COUNT

There are two ways to enlarge an image: add more pixels or make the pixels larger. Likewise, you can reduce an image's size by shaving off pixels or shrinking pixels. But shrinking and shaving are two different processes.

Shown in Figure 1 on page 233, *resizing* an image changes the size of its pixels, not its number of pixels. We're not increasing or decreasing the number of pixels, only changing how large those pixels are when printed. It's an inverse relationship: images with larger pixels will have a lower pixel density (fewer pixels in the same number of inches) when printed.

Shown in Figure 2 on page 233, *resampling* changes the image's size by increasing or decreasing its number of pixels. Images with more pixels will contain more information and often make for richer graphics.

Web design is concerned with resampling, not resizing, because every pixel in a web page will always be the same size. A web page that measures 800 pixels wide can accommodate images up to 800 pixels wide. Making every pixel wider doesn't change the fact that the layout can hold only 800 of them.

You can't make an image appear larger on screen by resizing its pixels because every pixel on the same screen will always be the same size.

RESIZING VS. RESAMPLING

1 *Resizing* an image changes the size of its pixels, not its number of pixels.

2 *Resampling* changes the image's size by increasing or decreasing its number of pixels.

1

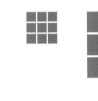

2

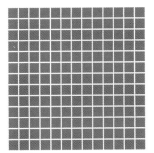

RESIZING AND RESAMPLING IN PHOTOSHOP

Photoshop's Image Size box (*Image > Image Size*) controls both the resizing and resampling of images.

The Resample checkbox changes how many pixels fit into a linear inch—literally the pixels per inch. If we turn off resampling, the only way to change the image's size would be to enlarge its pixels for printing. (See Figure 1 on page 235).

With the resampling box left unchecked, changing the Resolution box would alter the image's physical size when printed, but not its number of pixels. When printed, an image would appear larger or smaller. On a web page, it would be the same size. (See Figure 2 on page 235).

AN EXPERIMENT

Figuring out whether DPI matters in web layouts can be done by a little experiment. If we alter an image from 300p × 100p at 72dpi to 300p × 100p at 144dpi, how many pixels would we have?

1. Make an image 300 pixels wide and 100 pixels tall, at 72dpi.
2. Let's do some math. How many pixels would that be?
3. Now resize the image to 300p × 100p at 144dpi.
4. Let's do some more math. How many pixels is that?
5. The answers are:

    $300 \times 100 = 30,000$

    300×100 is still 30,000

RESIZING AND RESAMPLING IN PHOTOSHOP

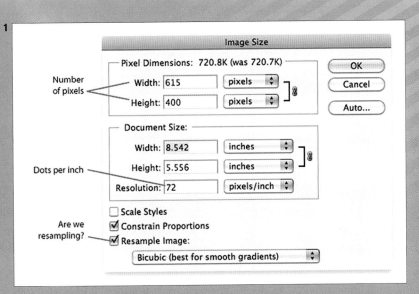

1 The Resample checkbox changes how many pixels fit into a linear inch—literally the pixels per inch.

2 With the resampling box left unchecked, changing the Resolution box would alter the image's physical size when printed, but not its number of pixels.

PIXELS PER INCH ON SCREEN

The number of pixels per inch is still relevant online, but DPI settings do not affect how an image is displayed.

Computer monitors can be physically measured in inches, and each displays a certain number of pixels. For example, let's say a 19" monitor shows 1280p × 1024p. The user could change it to display 1600p × 1200p, thus increasing its PPI (i.e., adding more pixels in the same number of inches). The important difference in print is that you can control an image's pixels-per-inch.

You can try this on most modern computers. On a Mac, go to *Apple Menu > System Preferences*, and then click on Displays to see the various resolutions at which you can set your monitor. For Windows, right-click on the desktop and select Personalize, and then choose Display Settings. Change the screen resolution (number of pixels) and watch as the items on your Mac or PC desktop get larger or smaller.

Obviously, your monitor isn't changing in size. But if you hold a ruler to the screen, you'll see that the size of icons and windows is *inversely* proportional to the number of pixels displayed. For example, a 13" laptop, a 17" CRT monitor and a 21" flat-panel monitor can all present a desktop that measures 1024p × 768p. More pixels mean smaller icons; fewer pixels mean larger icons. More pixels in the same monitor give you a higher pixel density; fewer pixels is lower. (See Figure 1 on page 237.)

The difference becomes more noticeable with other types of displays:

A digital billboard measuring 47 × 12 feet might use only 888 × 240 pixels (about 1.6 PPI).

PIXELS PER INCH ON SCREEN

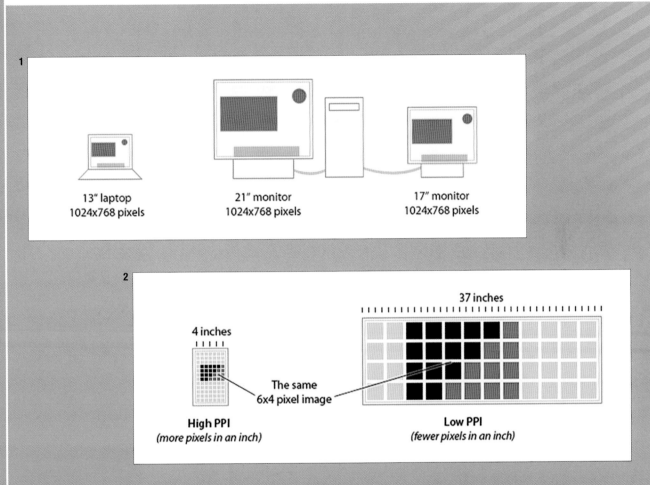

1 The size of icons and windows is *inversely* proportional to the number of pixels displayed.

2 A single PNG file measuring 100p x 100p would fit on both the 888p x 240p billboard and the 320p x 480p iPhone. But it would appear much larger on the billboard because the board's pixels are 100 times larger than the iPhone's (1.6 vs. 160).

An iPhone screen today measures 2 × 3 inches and holds 320 × 480 pixels (about 160 PPI).

A single PNG file measuring 100 × 100 pixels would fit on both the 888 × 240 billboard and the 320 × 480 iPhone. But it would appear much larger on the billboard because the board's pixels are 100 times larger than the iPhone's (1.6 vs. 160).

Figure 2 on page 237 shows two devices with different pixel dimensions.

The same image is being shown on two different displays. The differences in each display's PPI make the image on the right-hand display appear larger, even though it has fewer pixels overall.

You can test this yourself:

1. Create a JPEG that measures 960 × 100 pixels, at any pixel density.

2. Measure it by hand with a ruler.

3. Look at the same image on a computer with a larger or smaller monitor. For example, if you created the image on a 20" screen, test it on a 13" laptop.

4. Print the same number of pixels at different pixel densities to see different sizes on paper.

The result is that this one image would have the same number of pixels but a different width in inches. The website layout would appear in different sizes, despite identical code. (For an extreme case, look at the entire page on an iPhone; 960 pixels is fitted to three inches or less, without the file itself being changed.)

WHY 72 IS SIGNIFICANT

Many file formats, including JPEG, TIF and PSD, store an image's pixel density setting. If you save a JPEG at 200ppi, it will remain at 200ppi.

Other formats, including GIF and PNG, discard pixel density. If you save a 200dpi image as a PNG, it won't save that DPI at all. Many image editors, including Adobe Photoshop, assume that an image is 72dpi if the information is not stored. (Note: Photoshop's "Save for Web" feature discards unnecessary print information, including PPI from its Image Size dialog box.)

Seventy-two is a magic number in printing and typography. In 1737, Pierre Fournier used units called *ciceros* to measure type. Six ciceros were 0.998 inches.

Around 1770, François-Ambroise Didot used slightly larger ciceros to fit the standard French "foot." Didot's pica was 0.1776 inches long and divided evenly into 12 increments. Today we call them points.

In 1886, the American Point System established a "pica" as being 0.166 inches. Six of these are 0.996 inches.

None of the units ever strayed far from 12 points per pica: 6 picas per inch = 72 points per inch. It was an important standard by 1984, when Apple prepared to introduce the first Macintosh computer. The Mac's interface was designed to help people relate the computer to the physical world. Software engineers used the metaphor of a desk to describe the arcane workings of a computer, right down to "paper," "folder" and "trash" icons.

Each pixel on the original Mac's 9-inch (diagonal) and 512 x 342 pixel screen measured exactly 1 × 1 point. Hold a ruler to the glass, and you'd see that 72 pixels would actually fill 1 inch. This way, if you printed an image or piece of text and held it next to the screen, both the image and hard copy would be the same size.

But early digital pictures were clunky and jagged. As screen technology and memory improved, computers were able to display more pixels on the same size monitor. Matching a print-out to the screen became even less certain when raster and vector apps allowed users to zoom in and examine pixels closely. By the mid-1990s, Microsoft Windows could switch between 72 and 96 pixels per inch on screen. This made smaller font sizes more legible because more pixels were available per point size.

Today, designers and clients alike understand that the sizes of items on the screen are not absolute. Differences in screen size and zoom functionality are commonplace. But 72 is still the default.

HIGHER SCREEN PPI MEANS BETTER LEGIBILITY AT SMALLER POINT SIZES

Screens with higher PPI are great for legibility. More pixels per inch make letterforms easier to read. It also means that images and text must be larger (in pixels) to be readable. (See Figure 1 on page 241.)

The text sample has been resized from two different screen PPI settings. The top row has smaller pixels (i.e., a higher PPI on screen), so 8 points is the smallest legible font size. Text in the bottom row is barely legible below 10 points.

As PC monitors surpassed the pixel density of Mac monitors in the mid-1990s, websites built on Windows boasted smaller font sizes,

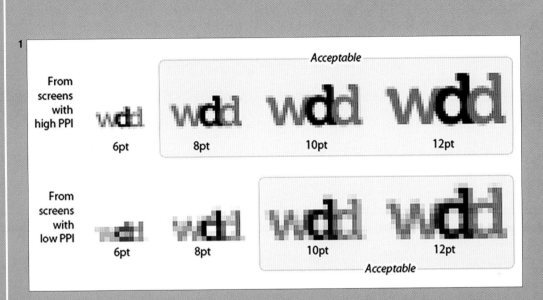

1 Screens with higher PPI are great for legibility. More pixels per inch make letterforms easier to read. It also means that images and text must be larger (in pixels) to be readable.

much to the dismay of Mac users. Today, screens for both platforms enjoy pixel densities high enough to make the differences moot.

Preparing images for the web means planning in pixels. If someone asks for a 2-inch graphic for the web, not for print, ask them, *"How big are your pixels?"* or even better *"How many pixels?"*

ABOUT BEN GREMILLION

Ben Gremillion is a web developer who thinks design is a process, not a product. You can learn more about him on twitter @benthinkin.

Technical Glossary

Designers branching out into web design or working with development teams absolutely must understand the jargon. I'm not saying you need to learn Drupal, but you should become familiar with common web concepts. While this technical glossary isn't exhaustive, it should give you enough background to get you going.

Accessibility: Accessibility is the consideration of a website's usability for those with disabilities, whether they have visual, hearing or physical impairments. Special consideration must often be made to ensure a website can be used by the entirety of its audience.

Affiliate program: An affiliate program is an Internet marketing tool in which an e-commerce website offers a commission to people who refer customers. Most often an affiliate gets a percentage of sales based on traffic referred to the site. Tracking is most often done using specialized software where affiliates use links containing extra data for tracking purposes.

AJAX (Asynchronous JavaScript and XML): AJAX is a way of building websites where the site changes and responds to what you're doing without having to reload the full page. Google Maps is a perfect example of this: The map changes and loads new content without refreshing the entire page. This creates a smoother user experience and is a common development technique.

Alpha transparency: This is when an image supports partial transparency (as in the PNG file format).

Each pixel of the image is assigned an alpha value, which represents its percentage of transparency. This percentage is multiplied by the color value of the pixel to determine its final color. This is incredibly important for placing images that require transparency over backgrounds.

Anchor: In a web page you can have links that point to other locations, or anchors, inside the current page. These are denoted by a pound symbol (#) in the link—a link such as http://yourdomain.com/page.html#chapter2 would point to the anchor named "chapter2" in the page.html file.

Application Programming Interface (API): An API is a way for programs to talk to each other. For example, Facebook has an API. It enables programmers to write code on their own website that can interact with Facebook directly.

ASP: ASP is an out-of-date server-side programming language created by Microsoft.

ASP.net: ASP.net is the modern version of ASP. It's also a server-side programming language.

Bandwidth: The term *bandwidth* is often used in two ways. It can refer to the amount of information that can be transmitted at one time. For example, your home Internet access speed is restricted by the amount of bandwidth you purchase—a 1MB data line can transfer 1MB of data per second. Or bandwidth can refer to the total amount of data transfer your web host provides for your website per month. For example, your host might limit you to 4GB per month. This means if your website exceeds a total of 4GB of data sent out over the course of a month, your site might go down or you might incur additional charges.

Below the fold: *Below the fold* refers the part of a web page that appears below the initially viewable area on a user's screen. So if a user's screen is 1024 × 768, they will see about 600 pixels above the fold. It's not the full 768p because you have to assume that part of the browser's framework and menus occupy part of the screen. What's above the fold is not a fixed number and can only be estimated. Common estimates for above-the-fold spaces include:

- 800 × 600: about 425 pixels above the fold
- 1024 × 768: about 600 pixels
- 1200 × 1024: about 850 pixels
- 1600 × 1200: about 1025 pixels

The terms *above the fold* and *below the fold* come from the newspaper industry—it refers to what's visible to the reader when a newspaper is folded.

Black hat SEO: This is the practice of engaging in search engine optimization tactics that seek to trick search engines into ranking pages highly. These tactics often backfire, as search engines will flag pages they suspect as using black hat SEO and bury them in the results.

Bounce rate: The bounce rate of a site is the percentage of visitors that view only a single page on your site before leaving. Single-view visitors are often considered an indicator of a problem. After all, the goal is typically to get people to stay on your site a while, not get out as fast as they can.

Breadcrumb: Breadcrumbs are a navigational tool that show where the current page of a website falls within its overall hierarchy. The breadcrumb usually links to each page in the trail so users can easily jump to the pages. A breadcrumb might look like: Home > Print Publications > The Web Designer's Idea Books > Volume 1.

Browser: A browser is the software you use to view web pages. On a desktop computer, this includes programs such as Internet Explorer, Firefox, Chrome and Safari. You even use a browser on your mobile device, even though it's usually not as clear that it's a separate piece of software.

Browser reset: Browsers render all website elements with predefined styles as set up by the browser manufacturers. Browser reset, a set of CSS codes within a website, undoes all of these styles so all browsers start from the same point. Web developers are split on the idea: Some see browser resets as an extra step that bloats the code, and others view it is a critical element.

CAPTCHA: CAPTCHA stands for Completely Automated Public Turing tests to tell Computers and Humans Apart. (That probably isn't much help, but you'll be a hit at parties.) In more practical terms, a CAPTCHA is a device used to detect if a human is completing an online form—like when you have to type a few bits of text from a scrambled image before you can submit a form. These little devices, despite how annoying they are, are incredibly important. Spammers love to target web forms and can use automated programs to fill out simple forms like a contact form over and over. A CAPTCHA can help protect you from getting hundreds or thousands of junk responses a day.

Cloud hosting: Cloud hosting is when multiple computers work together to create a single virtual computer. The advantage of this is that losing a single computer won't take down the whole system. Enormous applications such as Google operate on a cloud-like structure. But any website can be hosted on the cloud and enjoy the flexibility to endure huge traffic spikes.

Content Management System (CMS): A CMS allows multiple users to collaborate and publish content with ease. Such systems make it possible for content creators, editors and managers to update the content of a site without having to go through a developer.

Conversion: A conversion is when a user completes the tasks that the website was created to lead to. Most frequently this refers to an online purchase, but it could also include things such as completing a form, watching a video, visiting a specific page, signing up for a newsletter or any other goal.

Conversion funnel: The conversion funnel is the process a user must go through in order to complete a conversion. For example, on an e-commerce site, a user must:

- View a product
- Add it to their cart and view the shopping cart page
- Go to the checkout page
- Land on the confirmation page

A user that does all these things will have completed the conversion funnel. (It's referred to as a funnel because more people start it than finish it.)

Conversion rate: The conversion rate of a site is the percentage of visitors that complete a conversion as compared to the total number of site visitors. The higher the conversion rate, the better.

Cookie: A cookie is a small bit of information from a website that's stored on a user's computer. Developers use cookies to store information—this aids in maintaining user preferences, updating the contents of a shopping cart or tracking Internet usage.

CSS (Cascading Style Sheets): CSS is used to define the presentation of HTML, such as color, fonts and layout. With targeted CSS, the same HTML can be styled differently based on the output method (such as desktop computers, mobile or tablets).

CSS3: CSS3 is the third set of revisions to the CSS standards.

CSS framework: A CSS framework is a collection of pre-written CSS intended to speed up the development process. Frameworks often include predefined styles for things such as layout structures, grid systems, typography and browser resets.

Database: A database is used to organize data so it can be searched using server-side programming. Dynamic sites, such as e-commerce websites, store content in a database and then output the data as HTML.

Dedicated server: A dedicated server is a computer that's 100 percent dedicated to running your website(s). Large websites can pay for a full server to accommodate large amounts of traffic or specific components that must be installed on the server.

Deprecated: Software features or standards that are deprecated are no longer a part of the current specifications. For example, certain HTML tags have been deprecated as they are replaced with different tags. Deprecated HTML tags typically still work but are no longer the preferred tags.

DHTML (Dynamic HTML): DHTML is a combination of (often) HTML, CSS and JavaScript used to create interactive websites.

DNS (Domain Name System): DNS is a naming system for computers and servers used to translate domain names into IP addresses. Just as a GPS unit must translate an address into latitude and longitude, on the Internet, a computer uses DNS to look up the website's IP address.

Doctype: Doctype is short for Document Type Declaration and it tells a user's web browser what type of document it's viewing. More specifically, it associates the page with a specific Document Type Definition that should be used to render the page.

DOM (Document Object Model): The use of the DOM is most frequently associated with JavaScript, though its purpose extends beyond that. The DOM is the way JavaScript views and interacts with the elements of an HTML document.

Domain name: Domain names are used to define the location of a website on the Internet: www. examplesite.com. Domain names point to IP addresses, which specify the location of a server on the Internet. Domain names are the virtual-world equivalent to mailing addresses, which can be translated to latitude and longitude. Domain names make Internet addresses readable by humans.

DPI (Dots Per Inch): DPI refers to the number of dots per inch—it applies to printed mediums, not the web. (See also *Pixel*.)

Drupal: This is a free, open-source content management system and framework.

Dynamic web page: Websites once had to be coded page by page (these are referred to as "static" pages).

Dynamic websites automatically update content within the page structure.

Elastic design: A layout using elastic design bases its size on a relative unit rather than pixels.

Embedded styles: Embedded styles are CSS style definitions embedded in an individual web page instead of being stored in a separate and global file.

Entry page: The entry page of a site is the first one a user views. While the home page is a common entry point, users may enter anywhere in the site. The term *entry page* is most frequently used in site analytics.

Exit page: The exit page is the last page a user views on your site. Using analytics to determine exit pages tells you which pages of your site are losing visitors.

Extensible Markup Language: See XML.

External style sheet: An external style sheet file, which contains nothing but CSS, is typically used to create the styles for an entire website. This way the same file can be included in every page, allowing the styles to universally apply to the site.

Favicon: A favicon is a small image, usually 16 × 16 pixels, associated with a website. These images are displayed in many browsers' tabs or bars, and are often connected to bookmarks as well.

Fixed-width layout: A fixed-width layout stays the same regardless of the size of a user's browser. If users' screens or browsers are too small, they'll have to scroll to see the whole site. For many designs, fixed-width layouts are necessary in order to maintain control over the layout of the page in a browser.

Framework: A framework is a collection of pre-made assets that allow developers to build sites more rapidly without having to reinvent the wheel. For example, jQuery is a JavaScript framework, a huge collection of pre-written JavaScript. There are frameworks available for almost every coding language.

FTP (File Transfer Protocol): This is a way to transfer files over a network.

GIF (Graphics Interchange Format): This type of image is ideal for files that have few colors. A GIF file cannot have more than 256 colors in it, which makes it ideal for structural images that are based on solid colors. This format doesn't serve gradients and photographs well—see JPEG instead. GIFs can also contain multiple frames to create animations, a feature that has been used for both good and evil.

Graceful degradation: Also called *fault-tolerant design*, graceful degradation allows users with older browsers or operating systems to still access content.

Hexadecimal: Hex numbers are a base-16 number used for representing colors in web pages.

HTML (Hyper Text Markup Language): HTML is a language used to describe content. Tags—denoted by < and > symbols—wrap around content to establish its purpose.

HTML5: HTML5 is the fifth major revision to the HTML specification. It's built on the previous versions by deprecating some tags and adding others.

HTTP (Hypertext Transfer Protocol): HTTP is the protocol used to transfer data online. HTTP tells the user's browser how it's going to transfer information.

HTTPS (Hypertext Transfer Protocol over SSL): HTTPS is a secure, encrypted version of basic HTTP. For example, the credit card information you enter on an e-commerce site using HTTPS is encrypted before being transferred.

Image map: When an image on the web is designated as a hyperlink, you can click anywhere on the entire image to go to a single URL. But with an image map, you can point different areas of the image to different URLs.

Impression: An *impression* is an advertising term that refers to each time an ad unit (such as an image or a hyperlink) is displayed for a user to see (or "served").

Inbound link: An inbound link is any link from an external website pointing to your site.

Inline styles: Inline styles are placed in the HTML of a file directly on the elements as they appear in the page. It doesn't allow for any global changes to be made.

IP address: An IP address is a series of numbers separated by periods—such as 216.239.51.99—that's used to identify a computer on the Internet. Domain names are directed to IP addresses through DNS.

JavaScript: JavaScript is a programming language that runs in the user's browser. The code is embedded into a web page, downloaded to a user's computer and run within the browser (referred to as client-side code). JavaScript isn't the same thing as Java (which is a programming language), nor does it have any relationship to it. The primary purpose of JavaScript is to modify the HTML of a page dynamically.

JPEG/JPG: JPEG is a file format suited for photographs. JPEGs can contain a range of compression values, an optimal way to compress images for display online.

jQuery: jQuery is a library of helpful tools written in JavaScript. This popular library lets you easily modify the HTML and CSS of a page to make it interactive and dynamic. Learn more at http://jquery.com.

JSON (JavaScript Object Notation): JSON, an alternative to XML, is a simple format for exchanging data online. It's a language used by programs and generally isn't intended for users to view.

LAMP (Linux, Apache, MySQL and PHP): LAMP is a web development setup that accounts for the operating system (Linux), web server (Apache), database (MySQL) and scripting language (PHP), all the elements required to run a website. There are numerous options that can replace each of these individual elements, but the LAMP combination is pretty common and can run WordPress sites.

Liquid layout: A liquid layout is one that sizes automatically to fill the entire browser space. Such layouts require a great deal of flexibility, as things shift and move based on the width of the user's screen.

Metadata: Metadata is data used to describe other data. On the web, it most often refers to data in the header of a web page (an invisible part of the page structure), which is used to describe the contents of the web page. Search engines and other programs use metadata to identify the contents of a page. Google has publicly stated metadata is no longer used to rank pages, so it's now marginally important for SEO purposes.

Meta tag: A meta tag is the HTML tag used to store metadata in a web page.

MIME type (Multipurpose Internet Mail Extensions): The MIME type for a file tells the user's browser what application type should be used to display a file being transferred, such as an audio file or video file.

Minify: Minify is the process of shrinking code so that it takes up as little space as possible, ensuring that it can be transferred as quickly as possible. This is a common technique for making sites run as fast as possible, and there are many tools for minifying HTML, CSS and JavaScript. The only downside is that the resulting code can be much more difficult to read and edit.

MySQL: MySQL is a relational database management system that runs on web servers and stores numerous databases. MySQL (pronounced "my sequel") is necessary to run CMS tools such as WordPress and Drupal.

Natural search: A natural search (or organic search) is a search that produces results ranked based on the content they contain, in contrast to paid searches, which contain paid results.

Non-breaking space: A non-breaking space is a blank space character used in HTML to occupy space.

Open-source software: This is freely distributed software whose code is open to the public.

Organic search: See *Natural search.*

Outbound link: An outbound link is a hyperlink that takes users away from your site. (See also *Inbound link.*)

Pageview: Analytics tracks the number of times a specific web page was viewed. A pageview is registered each time a user loads the page in their browser.

Permalink: Permalink is short for permanent link. The permalink provides a permanent URL that can be used to find a blog post or web page.

PHP: PHP is a common server-side programming language. It is commonly associated with open-source software, such as WordPress and Drupal.

Pixel: A pixel is the smallest individual dot on a computer screen. The resolution of a screen is measured in PPI, or pixels per inch.

PNG (Portable Network Graphics): The PNG is very similar to the GIF, but it supports far more colors. Its most important feature in terms of web development is its support for alpha transparency.

Progressive enhancement: Progressive enhancement is a way of building web pages where the web page uses more and more features as the user's browser supports it. The most modern browser will use features that are simply ignored in older ones. Progressive enhancement is the reverse perspective of graceful degradation.

Quirks mode: Your web browser, in quirks mode, attempts to provide the most backwards-compatible environment for displaying websites. It doesn't strictly adhere to the most current specifications and instead accommodates for as many coding approaches as possible.

Registrar: A domain registrar is a company authorized to sell domain names.

Responsive web design: Responsive web design is an approach to building websites in which the page is built to adapt to or respond to the user's environment. A responsive site will render differently depending on the user's browser size and if they are using a tablet or smartphone.

RGB (Red, Green & Blue): RGB is a color model used on digital screens where red, green and blue dots are combined to create any color required.

RSS (Really Simple Syndication): RSS is data structured as XML and is used to transmit web content across the Internet. Programs use RSS to update and display data from external sources.

Search Engine Optimization (SEO): SEO is the process of optimizing web pages so that their appeal to search engines is maximized.

Selector: In CSS, selectors are used to identify the target of the styles being written. For example, you could use the selector "p" to target all paragraph elements. Very complex rules are available for targeting various HTML elements in a page.

Semantic markup: Semantic markup is HTML that's been written so the tags accurately describe the data they contain.

Server-side code: Server-side code is run on the server before the HTML is sent to the user's computer. Server-side code is used to render HTML dynamically: When the user requests a web page, a program on the server that stores the web files runs and generates the HTML before sending it to the user. Common server-side languages include PHP, Ruby, Java and ASP.net.

Shared hosting: Shared hosting is a web hosting option where many sites are stored on a single server. Most discount hosting plans are based on shared hosting.

SOAP (Simple Object Access Protocol): SOAP is an XML-based protocol used by computer programs to interface with other programs across the Internet.

SSL (Secure Socket Layer): SSL is a protocol used for transferring data and it's a critical component for securing web content as it's transmitted. Combined with HTTP, you get HTTPS.

Subdomain: A subdomain is an extension of a domain name that can respond to a distinct IP address. For example, if your domain name is yourdomain.com, a possible subdomain would be extra.yourdomain.com. This allows you to set up multiple sites from a single domain name.

TLD (Top Level Domain): A TLD is the last part of a domain name. This includes .com, .edu and .org, for example. Each country also has a TLD, such as .us for the United States, and .uk for the United Kingdom.

URL (Uniform Resource Locator): A URL is the address of a document on the Internet. For example, http://www.yourdomain.com/some-file.html.

Usability: Usability is the process of making a website easy to use by its visitors. Usability can be measured by analyzing conversion rates.

User agent: The term *user agent* most commonly refers to web browsers. It can also refer to other applications that retrieve content from web servers, such as screen readers and spiders.

Validate: Validating code (such as HTML, CSS and XML) is to check it against a standard to confirm it follows the rules established for the language.

W3C (World Wide Web Consortium): This organization sets the standards used online, such as HTML and CSS.

White hat SEO: White hat SEO is the legitimate and honest use of targeted content to achieve natural search engine results.

WYSIWYG (What You See Is What You Get): Any interface or system that allows you to edit content while previewing it is described as wysiwyg.

XHTML (Extensible HTML): XHTML is essentially HTML version 4.0. It can also be described as the XML version of HTML.

XML (Extensible Markup Language): XML is a way to store data in which you can custom define any tags that you need. XML looks a lot like HTML, but it's meant to store and transfer data that is ultimately translated into HTML for display online.

APPENDIX D
Further Reading

Despite my hopes of containing everything you will ever need to know about the web in a single book, I truly believe you can benefit greatly from reading some additional books. Below are some of my top recommendations on a wide variety of topics that impact the web and your job as a designer.

The Web Designer's Idea Book
Volumes 1 and 2 by Patrick McNeil
amzn.com/1600610641, amzn.com/160061972X

While it might feel like shameless self-promotion, if you find this book useful I am pretty sure you will find my inspirational series equally helpful. In fact, I like to think that this book complements the others very nicely.

Advanced Web Metrics With Google Analytics, 2nd Edition by Brian Clifton
amzn.com/0470562315

If you need to dig in and truly understand how to put Google Analytics to work, then this is the only book to get. You will be amazed at how much is possible with Google Analytics, and you will quickly discover why it is the most popular tool for tracking site traffic.

HTML5 for Web Designers by Jeremy Keith
www.abookapart.com/products/html5-for-web-designers

This brief book is invaluable for immersing yourself in the world of HTML5. There is literally no comparison when it comes to summing up a technical topic with such ease.

CSS3 for Web Designers by Dan Cederholm
www.abookapart.com/products/css3-for-web-designers
Another book from A Book Apart that will provide you with a lot of direction when it comes to working with CSS3. This brief book sums up the technology, what you need to know and how it applies to real world design.

Hardboiled Web Design by Andy Clark
http://hardboiledwebdesign.com
This beautiful book shows that books about code can not only be incredibly informative, but beautiful at the same time. *Hardboiled Web Design* will forever alter how you view and approach web development.

A Website That Works by Mark O'Brien
www.newfangled.com/a_website_that_works
This book covers the strategy behind building an effective agency website. But the ideas learned here easily transfer to countless other types of websites and situations.

Web Design for ROI by Lance Loveday and Sandra Niehaus
amzn.com/0321489829
The purpose of this book is to help you view your website as a business and learn how to maximize the return it creates for you. This book shows that web design is about more than making a site look good, it is about making it function.

Don't Make Me Think: A Common Sense Approach to Web Usability by Steve Krug
amzn.com/0321344758
If you want to learn more about usability, this is absolutely the place to start. This is one of the bestselling web books of all time and is a guaranteed way to get in touch with usability.

A Project Guide to UX Design by Russ Unger and Carolyn Chandler
amzn.com/0321607376
User experience is a fundamental yet often overlooked aspect of web design, and this book will help you dig into the topic.

The Design of Sites by Douglas K. van Duyne, James A. Landay and Jason I. Hong
amzn.com/0131345559
This is one of those books that is totally overwhelming at first because it is so rich with information that you can hardly handle it. However, if you want to learn what makes large sites work, nothing compares to this priceless book.

Above the Fold: Understanding the Principles of Successful Web Site Design by Brian Miller
amzn.com/144030842X
Above the Fold is a book about the fundamentals of effective graphic communication online, including layout and usability.

Permissions

p. 013 **www.doublediamondmoving.com** Jeff Woodruff © 2011
p. 013 **www.fullmoonbbq.com** Full Moon Bar-B-Que © 2011
p. 013 **http://alexanderhomesteadweddings.com** Bullman Design LLC © 2010
p. 014 **www.doopsuikerpoppies.be** Weblounge © 2011
p. 014 **www.moo.com** Moo.com © 2011
p. 014 **http://getconcentrating.com** © 2011 rocket
p. 017 **http://holyrollersfilm.com** First Independent Pictures © 2011
p. 017 **www.ryanedgarmusic.com** Ryan Edgar © 2011
p. 017 **www.bloedoranjegallery.com** Momkai © 2011
p. 018 **www.bloggercore.com** Arun pattnaik © 2011
p. 020 **www.inspiredology.com** © 2011 Projekt19
p. 020 **www.webdesignerdepot.com** WEBDESIGNER DEPOT © 2011
p. 020 **http://freelanceswitch.com** Envato © 2011
p. 022 **www.suffolk.edu/admission** © 2011. Suffolk University.
p. 025 **www.handsetdetection.com** Teleport Corp Pty Ltd
p. 025 **http://network.operationshower.org** Integrity © 2011
p. 025 **www.quoteroller.com** CodingStaff Inc. © 2010
p. 026 **www.cheshirescouts.org.uk** Cheshire County Scout Council © 2011
p. 026 **http://drleaf.com** Dr Leaf © 2011
p. 026 **http://themes.bavotasan.com** c.bavota © 2011
p. 030 **www.thefwa.com** The FWA © 2000-2011
p. 030 **http://patterntap.com** Squared Eye © 2011
p. 030 **www.designsnips.com** Brian Golatka © 2011
p. 033 **www.beautiful-email-newsletters.com** Spoiltchild.com Ltd © 2011
p. 033 **http://motionspire.com** The Wojo Group © 2011
p. 038 **www.giftsproject.com** Appchee Applications Ltd. © 2011

p. 040 **www.mindmeister.com** Copyright 2011 MeisterLabs
p. 041 **www.protoshare.com** Site9, Inc. © 2011
p. 048 **www.myimpact.co.uk** Impact Media Design © 2011
p. 048 **www.ambassadorsforlife.org** Church Media Group, Inc. © 2011
p. 048 **www.joshkennedydesign.com** © 2011 Josh Kennedy.
p. 050 **http://openpublicapp.com** Phase2 Technology LLC © 2011
p. 050 **http://bavotasan.com** c.bavota © 2011
p. 050 **www.actionforblindpeople.org.uk** Action For Blind People © 2011
p. 051 **www.webcoursesbangkok.com** Web Courses Bangkok © 2011
p. 051 **www.carolinagirlevents.com** Jonea Gene © 2011
p. 051 **www.mo.gov** Integrity © 2011
p. 054 **http://agencydivision.com** © 2011 Siska Flaurensia
p. 054 **http://ismaelburciaga.com** Ismael Burciaga © 2011
p. 054 **www.pegasus-opera.net** © 2011
p. 055 **www.firebratstudio.com** © Firebrat 2011
p. 055 **www.funarisedie.com** © 2011
p. 055 **www.smashapp.com** Dear Future Astronaut AB © 2011
p. 057 **http://migreyes.com** Mig Reyes © 2011
p. 057 **http://blog.vtravelled.com** John O'Nolan © 2011
p. 057 **www.teapot.cl** Teapot.cl © 2011
p. 058 **www.neuformat.com** NEUFORMAT Klaus Lehmann © 2011
p. 058 **http://hiddenriverevents.com** Bullman Design LLC © 2010
p. 058 **www.mccoy.co.uk** Rich McCoy © 2011
p. 061 **www.zivmeltzer.com** Ziv Meltzer © 2011
p. 061 **http://alliance-for-africa.org/** Alliance for Africa Assistance © 2011
p. 061 **http://missionhillschurch.com** Mission Hills Church © 2011

p. 146 **www.inflicted.nl** Copyright © 2011 inflicted

p. 146 **www.paradox-labs.com** Copyright © 2011 Paradox Labs

p. 148 **www.kymerastudio.com** Kymera © 2011

p. 148 **http://qualithemes.com** Mostash © 2011

p. 148 **www.stargraphicdesign.com**

p. 150 **www.carmodsaustralia.com.au/** Ziller © 2011

p. 152 **www.smashapp.com** Dear Future Astronaut AB © 2011

p. 152 **www.uploadify.com** © 2011 Ronnie Garcia

p. 153 **http://network.operationshower.org** Integrity © 2011

p. 155 **www.photopodapp.com** Dear Future Astronaut AB © 2011

p. 155 **www.cybay.de** © Cybay New Media GmbH

p. 156 **www.andrewckor.com** Andrew Ckor © 2011

p. 159 **www.w3roi.com** Awio Web Services LLC © 2011

p. 159 **www.handsetdetection.com** Teleport Corp Pty Ltd

p. 161 **www.superuserstudio.com** Super User Studio Ltd © 2011

p. 166 **http://authenticjobs.com** Authentic Jobs Inc © 2011

p. 173 **http://stlshopper.com** Integrity © 2011

p. 173 **http://kristaganelon.com** Krista Ganelon © 2011

p. 184 **http://swixhq.com** SWIX Inc. © 2011

p. 198 **www.dangrossman.info** Dan Grossman © 2011

p. 198 **www.pixelflips.com** © 2011 Phillip Lovelace - Pixelflips

p. 200 **http://davebrookes.com** Dave Brookes © 2011

p. 200 **www.futuretap.com** FutureTap GmbH © 2011

p. 200 **www.webcoursesbangkok.com** Web Courses Bangkok © 2011

p. 203 **www.markoprljic.com** Marko Prljic © 2011

p. 203 **www.creativitea.co.uk** Creativitea Ltd © 2011

p. 203 **www.andrewckor.com** Andrew Ckor © 2011

p. 205 **www.getsyncd.com** Remix Creative © 2011

p. 209 **www.drkrush.com** Derek Rushforth © 2011

p. 209 **www.colinmckinney.co.uk** Colin McKinney © 2011

p. 211 **http://scentsybuddy.com/** Scentsy © 2011

p. 211 **http://www.reading-riding-retrofit.org** Bullman Design LLC © 2010

p. 211 **http://daytonfarmersmarket.com** FOUND DESIGN + INTERACTIVE © 2011

p. 212 **www.brettnyquist.com** Brett Nyquist © 2011

p. 212 **http://authenticjobs.com** Authentic Jobs Inc © 2011

p. 212 **http://williamsnash.com** Williams & Nash. © 2011

p. 215 **http://karijobe.com** Kari Jobe © 2011

p. 216 **http://collisionlabs.com** Collision Labs, Inc. © 2011

Index

Check out these other great books from Patrick McNeil!

THE WEB DESIGNER'S IDEA BOOK

This is a handy desk reference for design layout, color and style that you will turn to again and again. Based on the author's website, DesignMeltdown. com, you'll find a huge collection of websites organized by a wide variety of criteria. You'll find examples of sites before they're redesigned and see multiple examples of the redesign. You'll find a treasure trove of visual inspiration—helping you to see what others have done and how you can adapt those ideas to your own needs.

THE WEB DESIGNER'S IDEA BOOK, VOLUME 2

Volume 2 of *The Web Designer's Idea Book* includes more than 650 new websites arranged thematically, so you can easily find inspiration for your work. The web is the most rapidly changing design medium, and Patrick McNeil offers an organized overview of what's happening right now. Sites are categorized by type, design element, styles and themes, structural styles and structural elements. This new volume also includes a helpful chapter explaining basic design principles and how they can be applied online.

Find these books and many others at MyDesignShop.com or your local bookstore.

For more news, tips and articles, follow us on Twitter: @HOWbrand

For behind-the-scenes information and special offers, become a fan of our Facebook page: facebook.com/HOWmagazine

SPECIAL OFFER FROM HOW BOOKS!

You can get 15% off your entire order at MyDesignShop.com! All you have to do is go to www.howdesign.com/howbooks-offer and sign up for our free e-newsletter on graphic design. You'll also get a free digital download of *HOW* magazine.